Pro Web Project Management

Justin Emond

Chris Steins

Apress®

Pro Web Project Management

President and Publisher: Paul Manning
Lead Editor: Ralph Moore
Editorial Board: Steve Anglin, Mark Beckner, Ewan Buckingham, Gary Cornell, Morgan Ertel, Jonathan Gennick, Jonathan Hassell, Robert Hutchinson, Michelle Lowman, James Markham, Matthew Moodie, Jeff Olson, Jeffrey Pepper, Douglas Pundick, Ben Renow-Clarke, Dominic Shakeshaft, Gwenan Spearing, Matt Wade, Tom Welsh
Coordinating Editor: Annie Beck
Copy Editor: Lawrence Hargett
Compositor: Apress Production (Brigid Duffy)
Indexer: SPI Global
Artist: SPI Global
Cover Designer: Anna Ishchenko

Distributed to the book trade worldwide by Springer Science+Business Media, NY., 233 Spring Street, 6th Floor, New York, NY 10013. Phone 1-800-SPRINGER, fax (201) 348-4505, e-mail orders-ny@springer-sbm.com, or visit www.springeronline.com.

For information on translations, please e-mail rights@apress.com, or visit www.apress.com.

Apress and friends of ED books may be purchased in bulk for academic, corporate, or promotional use. eBook versions and licenses are also available for most titles. For more information, reference our Special Bulk Sales–eBook Licensing web page at www.apress.com/bulk-sales.

Contents

About the Authors

 **Justin Emond** is a freelance web technology consultant. Justin has worked on both sides of the technology world, in internal technology departments and as an outside consultant delivering services to those on the inside. Prior to being a freelance web technology consultant, Justin was a consultant at Pantheon and a senior project manager at Urban Insight. He has also taught a variety of technology courses at the USC Viterbi School of Engineering, from web programming to project management. He occasionally writes at MissingFeatures.com on topics ranging from usability to interface design to project management. In addition to his work at Urban Insight and Pantheon, Justin created Droptor, a web application that helps teams manage sites powered by the Drupal content management system, and Droptopia, an online visual portfolio of expert Drupal agencies. Justin has a degree in psychology from the University of Southern California, and he regularly reminds Chris that USC is a far better school than UCLA.

 **Christopher Steins** is the chief executive officer of Urban Insight, Inc., a technology consulting firm based in Los Angeles. Chris has a decade of experience in technology consulting and urban planning. He has participated in all aspects of information systems life cycle development, including user requirements, project management, system design, development, and deployment. He has served as a consultant to public sector, state, county, and local agencies, Fortune 500 private firms, educational institutions, and nonprofit organizations. Chris is a lecturer at the University of Southern California, where he teaches a course on technology and public participation in government. Chris received his master's degree in urban planning and development from the USC School of Policy, Planning, and Development, and his bachelor of arts degree in English from the University of California, Los Angeles.

Together, Justin and Chris have managed more than 125 distinct web projects with budgets ranging up to $3 million for more than 60 different clients.

Acknowledgments

We would like to thank Danny Krouk, James Carberry, Alex Brazier, and the Apress editorial team for their help improving this book. Of course, any errors or oversights are solely our own.

I would like to thank my talented friends and colleagues at Urban Insight for creating an environment in which we are able to both innovate and learn from our mistakes. I especially want to thank Mindy Oliver, Abhijeet Chavan, Chun Wong, and Danny Krouk for their kind guidance and mentorship over the years.
—Chris Steins

I would like to thank all of my clients, collegeues, friends, and family for teaching me valuable lessons every day. I would also like to thank Alex Brazier for her unfailing support.
—Justin Emond

Introduction

Is This Guide for You?

This guide was written for those who will manage or fund technology projects with budgets between $25,000 and $500,000. Our goal is to provide a quick-start guide for professional, smart, competent people who are new to web project management, or who need some guidance on how to manage a web project.

- **This guide offers a practical, step-by-step project management process**. While it is adapted from best practices in the technology industry, this guide recognizes the differences in the size, scope, and cost of projects. Project management techniques that may work perfectly for a 3-year, $10 million project may be overly burdensome for a smaller but still important 6-month, $500,000 project.

- **This guide generally focuses on web application projects**. A *web application* is a software application that is accessed using a web browser over a public network, such as the Internet, or a private network.

If you are a project manager, this guide provides specific techniques and methods you can use to make your projects successful.

If you are a project sponsor or funder, this guide helps you plan for the types of work products you might expect to see during the course of your project. It also enables you to assist your team in developing practical and useful documents that keep your project moving in the right direction.

How Is This Guide Different?

Many books and guides espouse well-documented techniques for managing larger technology projects with budgets exceeding $1 million. Likewise, there are several excellent how-to guides for managing small web site development projects with budgets of less than $25,000.

Most projects, though, fall somewhere in between. The techniques, documents, and tools recommended for the highly ambitious projects—while impressive—are often impractical, and require far more overhead documentation than a midsize project of more than $25,000 and less than $500,000 is likely to need. In theory, many of the techniques applicable to small web site development projects also apply to midsize projects. However, techniques for small projects tend not to scale well when there are more than two project team members, and these techniques frequently do not recognize the complexity involved in a more challenging midsize project.

This guide is about how to manage a technology project with a budget generally between $25,000 and $500,000. It includes

- Examples from the authors' personal experiences;

- Examples of documents from real projects; and

- Immediately useful techniques that will translate to your own projects.

This guide **is not** an overview of popular project management methodologies and frameworks such as Agile and Waterfall, although we do touch on these topics.

Ultimately, we want this guide to serve as a reference that will help you to solve problems quickly and efficiently—problems that will inevitably arise in your own projects.

About the Document Examples

All of the example documents in this book are real, created by the Urban Insight team while working on projects for our clients.

Many examples are taken from a project with USC called the Annenberg Social News Platform (ASNP). The Annenberg School for

Communication and Journalism at the University of Southern California in 2009 decided to use the Drupal web content management system as the infrastructure for school-wide web publishing, student e-portfolio, and interactive media projects to provide real-life, hands-on journalism and communications experience to students.

The pilot news site for the ASNP is Neon Tommy. Neon Tommy is a web-only, Los Angeles-based news source sponsored by the Annenberg School for Communication and Journalism via the student-supported incubator program known as Annenberg Digital News. Neon Tommy offers news coverage about issues of concern to Southern California residents, but its audience is worldwide.

The Project Life Cycle

In this book, we make reference to various phases in the life of a project. These are the project phases and elements that are common to many, if not most, web development projects. The tips and techniques we offer are relevant to many phases in the project life cycle. For example, the section on how to run a meeting effectively will serve you well through your project, and perhaps even beyond your web project experience.

Following is a brief description of each phase, and where we discuss it in this book.

- **Planning**: This is typically the first phase of most projects, and involves outlining the full scope of the project. In some consulting organizations, this phase follows the approval of a proposal or scope of work. In many internal projects, the project begins with the planning phase. We define the conclusion of the planning phase with the client's approval of the wireframes, and requirements document. We discuss planning in Chapters 4 and 5.

- **Visual design**: This is often the most variable part of a project. In a web site development project, the design phase is often the area of the project where nontechnical team members have the most input, and where many smaller projects run over budget. Your best approach to keeping the visual design phase on track and on-budget is to produce an excellent requirements document and wireframes in phase 1. We discuss the design process in Chapters 5 and 6.

- **Development**: This is often the largest phase of the project, and where you have the greatest opportunity to be efficient, focused, and really allow your development team to stretch their wings. Conversely, this is also where you have the greatest opportunity to avoid the most dangerous mistakes from which most web projects suffer. Depending on the type and size of project, the development phase may start immediately after the planning phase, and conclude up to the testing phase. We offer lots of actionable tips and techniques on how to make this phase rewarding in Chapters 6, 7, and 8.

- **Content**: The content phase of the project often overlaps with development and testing. This is the phase where you engage your users or client to begin populating the system you're building with content or data. As part of this phase you also provide training to your client. Training is critical to the success of your project, but sadly is one of the most often overlooked areas of web projects. We discuss the content phase in Chapters 8, 9, and 10.

- **Testing**: When Chris first started running web projects, he felt guilty about having a section of the project and budget called "Testing" or "Quality Assurance." After all, when delivering a quality service or product, should it not be perfect? It's taken him many years to recognize that any project that does not plan for testing and quality assurance will not only fail, but fail spectacularly. Depending on the size of the project, quality assurance and testing can represent 5%–20% of the project budget. Check out Chapter 9 for an easy-to-follow guide for testing.

- **Launch**: Simply completing development or testing of a project does not define completion. It's useful to identify explicitly the discrete steps needed to launch a project successfully. We cover launching a web site in Chapter 10.

Additional project management responsibilities fall outside of the project process we outline here. In subsequent chapters, we also cover the following:

- **Defining the project**: Before a proposal is signed it must first be created. The task of turning initial, nebulous discussions with a client about a problem they face into a sensible (for both you and the client) proposal requires a thoughtful approach. We cover the process of defining a project in Chapter 2.

- **Meetings, meetings, meetings**: If there is one common theme that binds together the activities of a project manager, it is the meeting. Meetings can keep your project running smoothly as easily as they can devastate budgets and sap morale. We talk about how to run focused and efficient meetings that keep everyone happy in Chapter 3.

- **Support and operations**: Of course, launching the web site is only an intermediate step in the life cycle of your project. Now comes the really hard part: support and operations. Without a concrete plan for support and operations, even the most successful project can begin to degrade and cause pain. We cover how to make support and operations smooth in Chapter 11.

The Project Definition and Scope of Work

Before you have a project, you have a proposal. The project definition is vital because the proposal sets the tone for the entire life of the project. From our years of experience in advising clients on projects, we've developed the following simple approach to easily navigate the pre-project phase:

- What is the problem?
- Can we help solve the problem?
- Outlining the solution: the scope of work

Since the proposal is the first work product of yours that the client will see, it's vital to set a great first impression. With this in mind, we also cover how to prepare client documents.

Finally, we cover how to address a common client concern during the project definition phase: What is customization and what is configuration?

What Is the Problem?

Many years ago, when Chris was gracefully leaving the employment of a long-time entrepreneur to start his own business, his employer told him that he would not succeed.

"You won't make it. You don't have what it takes to make it on your own. You need to be able to sell wool blankets at a Dodger game on a hot summer day."

That remark hit Chris hard, especially coming from someone with whom he had worked for many years. But he also saw the fundamental difference in the way each of them would run a business.

He thought, "I won't sell blankets; I'll sell beer."

Chris often recalls this conversation when meeting with a new client. He asks himself, am I trying to sell this client something that they don't need—the wool blanket on a hot day? So when our team first speaks with a prospective client about a project, we present ourselves as advisors. We don't start by trying to sell a product or service. Instead, we learn about the client, their business, their technology, and their specific technology problem.

Be a Trusted Advisor

First, be an advisor. This approach will pay off down the road. If you appear to be a cheerleader for a particular technology or approach, your client will never be able to heed your advice without wondering if you are trying to promote your favorite technology. If you begin the project with an objective evaluation of the various approaches or technologies, you present yourself as your client's advisor or advocate. This is a much stronger position than being a promoter of a specific technology.

Tip When you hear your client's idea, rather than initially proposing a particular technology or solution, position yourself as an advisor and try to understand the client's problem.

Listen to what the client is telling you about his or her problem, and try to get to the root of that problem. Here is an example of how a conversation might start:

> Client: "We need a better system to print letters thanking donors for their contributions."

> Consultant: "Why, what's wrong with the current system?"

> Client: "It's too manual. We have to retype every-thing."

> Consultant: "What do you use to track your do-nors?"

> Client: "We keep some of it in a spreadsheet, and some of it in files."

If we had tried to solve this (admittedly simple) problem by recommending a system for printing letters, we would have committed ourselves to a specific technology without understanding the problem. **The problem here is not about printing letters. That is a byproduct of the real problem: the lack of a customer relationship management system or database.**

Here is another example of trying to use a one-solution-fits-all approach to problem solving. We know a highly technical and skilled colleague who is an expert with a programming language called Perl. When asked to complete a task or project, he will always use Perl. It does not matter if there is a better language or way to do the project; he knows Perl, and that is what he will use to solve the problem.

If we have a programming project for which Perl is a good choice, then he is an excellent fit. If we have a project where the requirements do not match what Perl offers, he is the wrong choice. He thinks anything could be done using Perl. But if Perl is not a good solution, you would not want him working on your project.

When you consider building a complex system or application, it is often unwise to select the system architecture and software based solely on the qualifications of a single person. Often, it is much better to evaluate several options and select the best fit.

Once we understand the client's problem, we usually offer three likely technology solutions, and present the pros and cons of each.

Be Honest. Really.

Being honest actually works very well. No one expects the project to go off perfectly. If you start the project by being honest about problems and concerns, you will be in a much stronger position to present problems as they arise during the course of the project.

If there is a less expensive way to do the project, identify it.

> Client: "We're thinking about asking you to imple-
> ment enterprise solution X to host and deliver
> streaming media from our web site."

> Consultant: "Hmm. That is a very good system, but it
> might be more than you need. Have you also consi-
> dered option Y?"

> Client: "No, I'm not familiar with option Y."

> Consultant: "Let's compare solutions X and Y, and
> see if Y might work you. It's about 10% of the cost of
> enterprise solution X."

> Client: "Great. Now we have plenty of budget to
> have you perform the evaluation."

Beyond the obvious ethical argument, honesty helps build a precious resource that is easily lost and painfully gained: credibility. Credibility built at
the start of the project—or even before it has begun—will help you manage
the inevitable challenges you will face later in the project. Even when it
hurts, it pays to be honest.

Can We Help Solve the Problem?

From time to time, when discussing a potential project with a prospective
client, we realize that the solutions we could bring to the table are not the
ideal options for the project. What do we do?

We discuss the most likely project options with the client, and then we tell
the client that we are unlikely to be a good fit because we are not experts
in the solutions that will best serve the project.

We are prepared to lose the business on that project. But, two surprising
things often happen:

- The client hires us anyway. Many clients appreciate the value of
  having an honest advisor on the project, so they will hire us to help
  specify the project, hire a consultant, or provide project
  management oversight.
- The client hires us for another project. Most organizations have
  multiple projects. Although you or your company may not be a

good fit for a particular project, the potential client is likely to remember your candor and engage you on a different project.

Like honesty, knowing when you are not a good fit for a project will help you build credibility. There is no short supply of vendors and partners ready to sell something to your client, but there is a shortage of honest people you can trust.

Outlining the Solution: The Scope of Work

If the client feels that we are a good fit the project, we're asked to prepare a scope of work.

Fundamentally, a scope of work is the statement about what you will do. Often, the scope of work includes a budget or expected level of effort. The scope of work sets the bounds on what will be included in the project, and importantly what will *not be included* in the project.

Scopes of work take many shapes, but the best of them have common elements. Your scope of work should almost always include the following:

Project Name

This is often an overlooked opportunity. Create an appealing and useful name that adds weight to the project. For example, "Admissions Database" is fine, but boring. Try changing the name slightly to "Admissions Database for Applicant Management," or "ADAM." Now the project has a catchy name, one that makes it seem more human, approachable, and manageable.

Contacts

Include the name and contacts of the project sponsor for whom you are preparing the scope of work as well as your own name and contact information.

Date and Version

A scope of work may go through several iterations before it is accepted. Add a date and the version of the scope of work so you know which version is current.

Background

Add a few sentences about the high-level business need for the project, as well as how it originated and other background information. While this information may be obvious to you and the project sponsor, you should be aware that a scope of work is often distributed well beyond the immediate project audience; for example, we know of a scope of work for a small web application development project that ultimately reached the CEO of a Fortune 500 company. This background clarifies the usefulness of the project to someone who is not familiar with the project.

Scope of Work

This is the essence of the project. Identify the different components or phases of the project separately. For example:

- Discovery and planning
- System architecture design
- Visual design

When we first started writing scopes, we would include one or more paragraphs about each project component. After observing how people tend to read scopes of work, however, we changed the way we prepare them. Typically, we try to include a **brief set of bullet points** that clearly define the work that will be performed and the products that will result from each step.

For example:

Discovery and planning

- Conduct a series of three kickoff meetings to identify requirements.
- Prepare a requirements document.
- Create the application home page wireframe.
- Create five wireframes of key functional pages.
- Update the project budget, if necessary.

In most cases, the project starts with an initial discovery and planning process (read more about this in Chapter 4). Clearly defining the steps you will use in each phase of the project and the specific deliverables helps set the client's expectations and limits what you will need to provide at each stage of the project.

This approach also makes it much easier to estimate an initial project budget. For example, it is very difficult to identify accurately how much time is required for discovery and planning, which encompasses many steps. If you break this down into discrete tasks, it is much easier to determine the time required for each component and to total these individual costs to arrive at a budget.

For example, instead of including a huge item like "development" that includes everything from design through launch, break up the scope and budget into smaller pieces that describe specific tasks included in development, such as

- Interface Theming
- Installation and Configuration
- Application Development
- Quality Assurance
- Testing and Beta Testing
- Launch

Timeline

Timelines will vary widely depending on the size of the project and the number of constituents. However, we find it helpful to prepare a generalized schedule as a starting point for discussion with the client. This schedule can typically be a simple Excel chart with five or six key milestones that correspond to key tasks in your scope of work. We usually include the following statement with the schedule:

"The project manager will update the project schedule upon completion of the discovery and planning phase of the project when the full project details are known."

This helps you define a general schedule while allowing you to defer building a detailed schedule until you have more information about the project.

Investment Budget

This is probably the first section that most people will turn to when looking at a scope of work. The investment budget section typically reduces the entire scope of work to an easily readable chart that includes each of the steps and the amount of time involved.

Tip Our rule of thumb is that if the project is around $7K, you usually present the time required for each task in hours. If the project is over $7K, you present the time required for each task in days. Trying to estimate the number of hours required for a project over $7K implies a level of precision in estimating that seldom exists in reality.

In many cases, your budget will be higher than what your sponsor expects. (Development is hard work!) If so, it helps to separate the optional tasks from the required tasks. You can do this easily by creating two budget sections: core project budget and optional project budget. This way, the project sponsor or client can immediately identify which aspects of the project can be moved into a later phase without disrupting the entire project.

This also helps to avoid having to answer questions like, "Can we move the discovery and planning task to phase 2?" Obviously the discovery phase must come before—not after—the start of the project because by definition, it's discovery.

Approval

Even in informal or internal scopes of work, include an approval section with signature blocks for the project manager or representative of the company, as well as the project sponsor or client. There is a psychological difference between verbally agreeing to proceed on a project and actually having to put your signature and name on a scope of work.

The scope of work should never be a replacement for a formal contract for services between an organization and a consultant. A contract protects both the consultant and the organization paying for the project in the unfortunate case where the project does not work out as intended and needs to be terminated, or in cases where the sponsoring organization needs to terminate the project due to budget or other considerations.

Don't Go Chasing Methodologies

Before going any further, we want to mention that this book is not about a specific methodology. If a project is poorly managed, it is at risk of failure regardless of whether Agile or Waterfall methodologies are used. **We don't have a methodology to sell you. We have a project to complete on schedule, on budget, and according to your expectations. If anything, we advocate a pragmatic approach to the use of methodologies.**

If you work in a larger organization that has a well-defined project management process, you may have little choice about which methodology your organization will use. However, for many project managers in web application projects, little thought is given to which, if any, methodology will be used. There are loads of software development methodologies floating around these days. Two of them seem to be exceptionally popular at present.

In the Agile software development methodology, teams work in short spurts building just a few features at a time, test and refine often, and gather feedback from the client frequently. Proponents of the Agile method argue that this helps to ensure client satisfaction as they are involved with the project from the start, and development can't drift away from what the client wanted.

The polar opposite of Agile development is the Waterfall approach, wherein you move from one defined step of the project to the next in a deliberate and orderly way.

Because the Agile approach includes so much more feedback from the client than the Waterfall approach, Agile development is often considered client-driven.

Several popular businesses are outspoken about this approach, and so the Agile methodology is often perceived as hot and young, while the Waterfall methodology is seen as stuffy and old. Think Facebook (hot, young, and exciting) vs. IBM (staid, fatherly, and predictable).

Hype and popularity are not valuable measures of the merits of a technology.

Tip Just as you would not select a technology for a project based on its popularity, you should not use a development method just because it is popular. Use a development methodology because it fits the requirements for the project.

Still, you will find that the approach we advocate in this guide is oriented more toward Waterfall.

Here are some pros and cons of each style based on our experiences:

Agile Methodology

Pros

- **Fast ramp-up**. If you have a tight timeline and a team ready to go, an Agile process can get you started developing an interim product within a few days of the project start.
- **Immediate results**. Agile focuses on providing immediately useful components during each sprint. If your project will benefit from being able to interact with and test drive the system quickly, Agile can work well for you.

Cons

- **Client expertise**. In a client-driven consulting process, Agile assumes that the client possesses expertise in areas that would be useful throughout development. If this is not the case, and the client is not technologically sophisticated, inconsistent or undirected feedback can hurt the project. Getting feedback from someone never involved in a web project before—let alone a consulting engagement—could prove to be a disaster.
- **Project delays are highly disruptive**. In our experience, many small and midsize projects are spread over long periods, and team members focus intermittently on the project in short bursts of time. In this case, if Agile is used, you can burn through your project budget quickly without achieving your project goals.

Waterfall Methodology

Pros

- **More structure**. The Waterfall methodology often provides a more structured approach to uncovering requirements at the beginning of a project. If the project has interrelated complex requirements and needs to be developed as a complete package, Waterfall tends to work best.

- **Manages expectations**. Using a well-defined Waterfall process can help manage the expectations of the client. You make it clear when feedback will be collected and include time to act on that feedback, make refinements, and respond to your client's concerns.

Cons

- **Changing requirements**. Since there is a defined lag in time between approval of project requirements and the client's first review, it's possible that new requirements have been identified or priorities have changed. In Waterfall, these are hard to address.
- **Planning time**. If you use Waterfall, you will spend significantly more time in project planning at the beginning of a project. This contrasts with Agile, in which the client and developer uncover requirements as the team proceeds with the project.
- **Less real-time feedback**. Typically, there are longer intervals between client feedback on a project managed using Waterfall than on a project managed using Agile. Some project managers mitigate this concern by demonstrating to the client incremental features or having guided "walk-throughs" of selected features of the application.

The Document Formats Rule

There are really three document formats:

- Formal, for documents like a scope of work or a requirements document;
- Informal, for a recommendations document or technology research summary; and
- E-mail, for everything else.

A formal document should have your logo, a nicely formatted footer at the bottom of the page, and a cover page with the client's name, project name, client contact, document date, and a document reference code.

Use this format for proposals, scopes, and requirement documents (where you do formal requirements gathering). But do not overuse this format. For example, if you are preparing a list of recommendations for server and site improvements on a project you are now supporting but did not build, the informal format will work fine.

The informal format is great for documents that are too long for e-mail but do not need the logo, branding, and client information. Still, these should have a simple footer with a page number and the document title.

Preparing Client-Ready Documents

Whether it is a requirements document, a scope of work, a list of recommendations, or a feature request list, documents sent to the client must be treated with care. Like it or not, the content of your e-mails and documents largely shapes the client's opinion of you. That is why a spelling mistake in an e-mail is so embarrassing—or should be. (See the "Tips for Writing E-mails" section in Chapter 8 for more information.)

Still, it can be painless to prepare client-ready documents. Follow these guidelines:

Send PDFs

Do not send documents in an editable format unless you specifically want the client to edit a document, which should happen infrequently. As a PDF, it looks more finished and works on any operating system or device.

Hand-Edit Your Document

The best way to edit a document is by hand. When you feel the document is complete on the computer, print out a copy, push your mouse and keyboard away, grab a pen, and edit the entire document, start to finish. When you find errors, mark them on paper—avoid jumping to the computer to fix them.

You will catch more errors and the prose will read much better after a hand edit. Just try it.

Double-Check the Attachment

When you send the document to your client, open the file you attached to the e-mail and briefly look it over. You will often catch overlooked errors this way; for example, when you finished editing you might have changed the orientation to landscape, resulting in an incorrect alignment of the page numbers in the footer. Then there are the Friday afternoon errors, like attaching the wrong file.

Configuration vs. Customization

These two words sound similar enough. However, they can imply a huge difference in your project's budget, level of effort, and timeline.

We find that when a current or potential client with a limited budget begins to outline ambitious plans for a project, explaining the difference between these two options can be useful.

In the simplest form, from a technical perspective, customization requires changing source code, while configuration does not.

Let's dig into the differences a little more deeply.

Configuring Software

You modify the software using the software's standard interface. For example, if you were using a web content management system, configuring the software would be completed using the web interface. Most good web-based software today is highly configurable, enabling you to shape the behavior of the software.

Customizing Software

You modify the code that powers the software. Customization can increase the cost and complexity of a project dramatically:

- You need a developer or engineer who understands the software and programming language well enough to perform the modifications.
- You have to **test the modifications** you have made to the software to evaluate how they will work with other parts of the software. If your customizations are extensive or if the software is very complex, testing can be at least as challenging as the customizations themselves.
- You have to **maintain the customization** to the software. When new versions of the software are updated, you will need to carry your customizations forward. Maintaining customization requires

you to have good documentation, a system to manage your code, and a developer who has expertise with the software.

Some types of software plan for customization and provide architecture to support it. For example, the open source web content management system, Drupal, provides a modular architecture in which you can write your own custom modules that interact with the software. When it comes time to upgrade, you know that all your code customizations are retained in a specific custom module.

- Customization projects tend to create consultant lock-in, as those who make custom refinements are the experts on how to maintain them.
- Finally, if you customize your software, future development and maintenance will cost more. For example, when we come into a project where there has been a lot of customization (particularly if this customization took place over a span of a year or more and with several developers), we expect that there will be a variety of problems with the testing, code, or documentation.

Despite the challenges, however, there are compelling reasons to customize software:

- Customizing software is typically far less expensive than writing new software. If an open source software product provides you with 75% of the functionality you need, customizing the software is likely to be significantly less expensive than writing new software from scratch.
- Why? Let's say you decide to rewrite an open source solution that provides 75% of what you need. You only have to do the work to recreate that 75%, right? Wrong. You will also need to fix all of the bugs and architectural issues that will naturally be introduced in the process of rewriting that code. Like it or not, more time is spent fixing bugs than writing software.
- From a marketing perspective, if you are supporting your products anyway, "customization" can make a nontechnical client feel good. People tend to like the idea of customizing—think about customizing your car, bike, wardrobe, and so forth. You offer your client the sense that he is special and you are building something just for him.

Cost Implications

When a client or potential client understands the difference between customization and configuration, she appreciates the features that may be required in the two types of software. She is much more understanding of the budget involved when the project requires customization.

Tip Our rule of thumb is to budget four times as much for customizing software than for configuring it.

Tactically, these cost implications can be used to help clients be sure that the incremental value they receive from a customization matches the cost. Some clients will ask for expensive customizations, but fail to notice that, of their requested customizations, two out of three were nice-to-haves, whereas one was worth many, many times its cost.

Wrapping Up

By this stage in your negotiations you should have a good general sense of what problem the client faces and whether you are a good fit to help address it. You should have all the tools necessary to write a great proposal. The next stage in the process—discovery and requirements—is to detail all of the specific features and functions of the project. We cover this in Chapter 4.

However, before we dive into discovery and requirements, we will spend the next chapter looking at a vital project management activity that occurs at all stages of the project process: meetings.

If project management is three things, it's about managing your team, your client, and your boss. It's in meetings where a lot of that "people management" happens. Bad meetings can be boring, unproductive, and inefficient. They can also put projects at risk if the client loses confidence in your ability to lead the project. Running a great meeting is vital to project management.

In the next chapter, we tell you about a disastrous meeting one of your authors attended and we give you real tips and tricks you can use to run efficient meetings that don't bore and do build client confidence. Read on!

Meetings, Meetings, Meetings

Meetings matter. Your participation in meetings is often the most visible aspect of your role as a project manager. Your ability to manage meetings and use them to your advantage will make a tremendous difference in the success of the project.

We'll start with a cautionary tale about how not to conduct a meeting, and use the takeaway points from that story to discuss issues related to running a successful meeting. Beyond general advice, we'll cover a few specific types of meetings that you are likely to encounter as a project manager, such as a project kickoff meeting.

We include tips on how to run a great meeting and how to write an agenda. To wrap up, we talk about how—*wait for it*—to wrap up a meeting.

Don't Do This: A Disastrous Kickoff Meeting

Greg is a client manager for a database consulting firm that won a large contract from a government agency to develop a database system that will track available jobs in the region. Greg has a decade of previous experience as a "change management specialist" working for a large telephone monopoly.

Greg is excited about this first opportunity to flex his project management muscles for his new employer; he was hired specifically for this project just a few months ago.

Before the kickoff meeting with the client, he met with the technical staff at his consulting firm, who gave him a crash course in the pricey database management software that his firm sells and configures. Greg is ready to go—ready to manage the client and run the project.

On the day of the kickoff meeting, Greg and his two "technical liaisons"— who will make sure he can field any technical questions that might get thrown his way—have trouble finding parking and arrive 15 minutes late. Fortunately, the meeting has been scheduled for 4 hours, so Greg shrugs off the lost time as trivial.

Greg makes a good showing introducing himself and his developers to the eight people from the client's agency who are attending the meeting. He is surprised that there are so many people; he anticipated only two or three. Although Greg did not bring an agenda, he has several company brochures, which he passes out and advises people to share. Fortunately, he has plenty of business cards, so he gives everyone one of those, leaving a few extra in the middle of the table for good measure.

There is some initial confusion about who is running the meeting. Greg is confident and announces that he is happy to lead the meeting. Since his background is in change management, he begins the meeting with an impromptu discussion about how technology can be an important tool for change.

After about an hour, Greg decides it is time to have the client begin describing what they want this new database system to do. Greg loves to talk, and at various points shows off his new database experience by explaining how databases work and why some of the client's ideas may not be so great.

Just when Greg thinks the conversation is really getting going, one of the client's representatives, Bill—whom Greg has decided he does not particularly like because he asks a lot of pointed follow-up questions—asks Greg to define the process that will be used to develop the database system.

This sounds suspiciously like a technology question, so Greg asks one of his developers to answer. After all, technology is not Greg's specialty. The developer launches into a lecture on database management systems, schemas, triggers, stored procedures, normalizing data, and even database security and management. Greg thinks this is great stuff and takes a few technical notes in his leather-bound notepad so that he is more prepared to discuss the process next time.

After 3 hours, Greg notices that some of the clients are slipping out of the room and others are checking e-mail on their smartphones. Ah well, Greg thinks, they cannot be expected to understand all the technical details, or why would his firm have been hired in the first place? Greg decides that the group needs a break and interrupts one of the client representatives to announce that they will take a 10-minute recess before wrapping up the last portion of the meeting.

After the break, only two of the client's representatives have returned, and Greg decides to use the time to plan out the next meeting. He feels as if this meeting has gone very well and would like to plan another 4-hour meeting for the following week so they can continue making good progress. The client's representatives seem hesitant to commit to another meeting, but Greg reminds them that change is never easy, and there is still a lot to get done. Greg says that he will discuss with the developers what they want to cover in the next meeting, and he will probably set up a demo of the database software they use.

About 30 minutes past the scheduled end of the meeting, Greg tells the client that they are done for the day, gathers up his developers, and heads out to the car. He cannot wait to talk with the developers on the ride back to the office about what a great meeting it was.

When Greg gets back to the office, he rushes into his boss' office to give her the exciting news about how well the project is going. Greg is quite shocked to learn that the client has already called his boss and put the project on hold pending a discussion about how the project is being managed.

Although the names have been changed, this is a true account. Greg is a real person, and this meeting really did happen. Greg is a fine fellow, and someone you might enjoy having a beer with after work. However, Greg is totally unqualified at this stage of his career to be a project manager on a project of this size, complexity, and magnitude.

What did Greg do wrong?

- He arrived late.
- He failed to run the meeting.
- He let the meeting run too long.
- He didn't provide focus during the meeting.
- He didn't set a clear agenda or goals for the meeting.

This chapter introduces the fundamentals of running a successful meeting—including critical kickoff meetings and everything Greg did wrong—so that you can be successful and impress your colleagues and clients.

Project Kickoff

The kickoff meeting sets the tone and expectations for the balance of the project. Whether the participants are internal stakeholders or clients, this meeting will demonstrate the level at which the other team members are expected to perform.

For this reason, preparing well for your kickoff meeting is essential. Our three rules for running a kickoff meeting are as follows:

- **Prepare!** This means knowing who is coming to the meeting and what roles the participants have in the meeting. Be sure you have a solid agenda, and have the client approve it.
- **Start on time; end on time**. With a new client, this is very hard as the relationship is very new. You don't want to leave an unhelpful first impression and you do want to be respectful of your client. However, it is even more important to end the meeting on time. We find it is more effective to table unresolved issues and stay on track than to let unresolved issues derail the meeting timeline and agenda.
- **Run the meeting**. This is very hard for new project managers. Running a meeting does not mean that you have to rule with an iron fist, but it does mean that you have to gently keep everyone focused and moving forward on the agenda.

Now let's look at some of the logistics and planning that go into preparing for a kickoff meeting.

What Should Be Covered?

The goal of a kickoff meeting will vary slightly depending on the client and how many people are participating. In some cases, the meeting is to introduce the project to key stakeholders and gather high-level feedback. In other cases, it is to gather specific requirements about the project. Read more about this phase in the discussion of requirements documents in Chapter 4.

One Hour or Five Days?

The length of your kickoff meeting should correspond to the size of the project. If you have a large, complex development project, you may need 2 to 5 days. If you have a small web site project, you may only need 2 hours. You should let the agenda drive the length. However, keep in mind that people have difficulty concentrating for extended periods of time. Most people can only sit still for about 90 minutes. Therefore, when we create our agendas, we make sure that we have a break every 90 to 120 minutes.

For example, if we were organizing a daylong kickoff meeting, we would arrange meeting times along the following lines:

> 09:30 a.m. – 10:45 a.m. Session 1
>
> 10:45 a.m. – 11:00 a.m. Break
>
> 11:00 a.m. – 12:15 p.m. Session 2
>
> 12:15 p.m. – 01:30 p.m. Lunch
>
> 01:30 p.m. – 02:45 p.m. Session 3
>
> 02:45 p.m. – 03:00 p.m. Break
>
> 03:00 p.m. – 04:15 p.m. Session 4
>
> 04:15 p.m. – 04:30 p.m. Wrap-Up

If you start a meeting at 9:00 a.m., client representatives will almost always arrive late.

Tip Most people appreciate starting the meeting a little later so they have time to get into the office and check e-mail.

This type of schedule naturally breaks up the meeting into chunks, so if one session falls behind, you can shelve the unresolved topics and move into the next agenda session. The wrap-up session from 4:15 to 4:30 p.m. enables you to briefly summarize all the outstanding issues and identify the next steps. Having a wrap-up period helps everyone to understand that the day was successful and feel closure, even if there are unresolved issues.

How Big?

The ideal size for a productive kickoff meeting is two to six people. If more people participate, your level of productivity will drop. If there are more than ten people, it is likely that the meeting is more about introducing your team and capturing very high-level stakeholder feedback. This is OK, but make sure you know your audience. With ten or more people, you will want to keep the agenda very simple and focus on high-level feedback. Save the details for a small, more focused meeting.

Traveling for a Big Project?

If you will be traveling a long distance—for example, to another state—for your kickoff meeting, then hold one or more—pre-kickoff meeting planning calls or meetings. The goal of these initial meetings is to reduce the pressure during the formal kickoff meeting by ensuring that you identify the client's concerns, understand the key issues, and prepare an appropriate agenda.

For a major project with a client in Chicago (we are based in Los Angeles), we had a 2-day kickoff meeting scheduled. However, 2 weeks prior to the meeting, we held a series of three 1-hour calls with the client's project manager to go over the proposed agenda and identify several key goals. During this meeting, we discovered that the client was using two software systems with which we were unfamiliar. This allowed us to research the technical details about these systems beforehand, and as a result we were prepared during the meeting. These calls also helped the client's project manager feel more comfortable working with us and made sure that she would not be surprised during the meeting.

While this would have been inconvenient even if we weren't traveling such a distance, at least we could have rescheduled the meeting more easily rather than have wasted a long trip to do so.

If you are traveling more than 2 hours for a meeting that starts before 10 a.m., you should always drive or fly in the night before and stay in a hotel. There are simply too many things that can go wrong the morning of your meeting if you are traveling a long distance. Plus, if you have arrived the night prior, you will be much more relaxed and calm during the meeting.

Preparing for a Meeting

If you do appropriate planning, your meeting will be much more likely to be successful. In this section, we give you a checklist of things you would typically do when planning a meeting.

Tip Seventy-five percent of the effort involved in the meeting should be completed prior to the meeting so that very little is left to chance.

- Send a meeting agenda and any materials at least 1 day prior to the meeting (see the next section, "Don't Waste Time: Write an Agenda").
- Clearly identify your goals (ideally at least one, and no more than three) for the meeting.
- On the evening before or the morning of the meeting, send a brief reminder, including the agenda and time, date, and location.
- Know who will be attending the meeting, include them on the agenda, and know at least a little (title, responsibilities) about each person. Ideally, **try to guess what will be important to the other people** in the meeting.
- If you are presenting one or more agenda items, know what point you will make with each item, and the result you want after presenting it.
- Arrive 5 or 10 minutes early to the meeting location to set up, including placing the agendas, powering up your laptop, and otherwise preparing.
- Bring copies of the agendas and all handouts. If five people are slated to attend the meeting, bring six copies of everything. That way, you won't be caught short if an extra person shows up.
- If you are demoing anything on your computer, have it loaded in advance. For example, if you are showing web sites, the various web pages should be loaded in different tabs, or your PowerPoint should already be running **before** the meeting starts.
- If your demo requires an Internet connection, have a backup presentation—it can be a simple set of screenshots—prepared in case of Internet problems, because you will have Internet problems.

- Beyond Internet connectivity, confirm in advance that the facility has everything you will need for your meeting. Don't assume anything.

Don't Waste Time: Write an Agenda

Meetings for small projects need to be efficient because your most scarce commodity is time to work on the project. In a larger project, however, you are likely to have more meetings involving more people simply because you have more stakeholders, a larger scope, and larger technical decisions to make. But meetings for larger projects—while more frequent and perhaps longer—need to be just as efficient, focused, and thoroughly planned as smaller project meetings. With a larger meeting, your stakes are higher.

Too many meetings without clear resolution are a wasted effort because discussions end up being circular or branching off into unintended areas. In either case, the discussion never addresses the meeting goals, and the participants' time is wasted.

Why bother running a good meeting? Because the old adage is true: time is money.

Tip When you are considering calling for a meeting, remember that in software, time is bugs: time spent in meetings is time not spent fixing bugs.

Try this little exercise to see just how expensive meetings are.

- At the next meeting you attend, make a mental note of how many people are involved.
- If you work at a consulting firm, calculate the hourly rate of each person and total the cost.
- If you work at a traditional software development firm, assign two bugs per programmer, and one testing document and three e-mails per project manager or architect at the meeting.

How much did your meeting cost? Was it worth what was achieved? A 2-hour meeting with three .NET developers, a database developer, a project manager, and a database architect just cost the firm eight bug fixes, two testing documents, and six e-mails to clients.

If the team bills at $200/hour, that meeting cost $2,400. *Ouch.*

Meetings are expensive, and most people hate them. Most people hate meetings because most meetings are not productive and are run poorly. But meetings do not need to be hated. It is not hard to run a great meeting. However, it does require planning, an agenda, and **clear goals**.

Why Do I Need an Agenda?

The whole point of a meeting is simple: to make a decision that involves more than one person. This decision might be a set of features, a schedule, an upgrade plan, or a technical outline to solve a problem. Whatever you might need from the meeting, it is still a decision.

Where does the agenda come in?

In order for a meeting to come to a decision, you need to have a clear goal. Why?

- A goal makes it clear to all involved what needs to be determined by the end of the meeting.
- A goal enables all participants to evaluate the success of the meeting.
- Most importantly, the goal leads to a decision.

So what does the agenda do?

The agenda makes the goal clear (by stating it succinctly in the agenda) and it sets a framework for writing the discussion topics so that they help attain the ultimate goal of the meeting: the decision.

The Agenda Clothing Rule

There is no set format for an agenda and no hard-and-fast template that you can apply to every kind of meeting. An agenda can be a simple three-item list sent to the team in an e-mail, or a full and formal two-page agenda as a PDF attachment in an e-mail sent to a client.

Tip The trick to selecting an agenda format is the *agenda clothing rule:* the format of the agenda should match the attire of the meeting attendees.

If you are meeting with clients who are wearing pressed pants and ties, you need a nicely formatted, formal agenda. If you are meeting with a development team wearing flip-flops and wrinkled T-shirts with trite, trendy statements, a simple e-mailed agenda will probably do just fine.

The short agenda—for the informal meeting—is usually written as part of a meeting reminder e-mail and contains a one-line goal for the meeting and a short list of two to five discussion items. It is short, sweet, targeted, and informal.

The long agenda—for the more formal meeting—is usually a full-page PDF that contains a few parts:

- Document title;
- Meeting location;
- Meeting date and time;
- Meeting goal(s);
- Topics/discussion items; and
- List of participants with titles and affiliations.

If the more formal meeting is meant to be more than an hour, you probably want to include times for each discussion topic. This helps you end circular discussions for items that are not making progress toward a decision in order to "respect everyone's time and move on to the next item."

If you had listed 30 minutes for the current topic and time is clearly up, it becomes easier to say, "I want to respect everyone's time, so I think we really need to move to the next topic," without offending anyone.

A long agenda should probably end with a "next steps" topic to allow the person running the meeting to wrap up and outline **what happens now**.

Topics, Topics, Topics

The core of any agenda is the discussion topics you outline. These should be easy to write if you have identified a goal for the meeting.

Here are a few points to keep in mind:

- Items **should be very short**—usually less than seven words (the thought process that goes into watering down a complex issue to just a few words tends to make clear the core issue that should be discussed);

- Be as **specific as possible** in each topic (the more vague the topic, the more vague and unhelpful the discussion will be); and
- Ensure that each topic helps achieve whatever goal you have outlined for the meeting.

One trick to determining what topics are achievable in the meeting is to take a moment and think about all of the immediate decisions you need to make for the project to continue. Think through the major work tasks you plan to assign to various members of your team, the next major project phase (and what you need to get there), and what work product you might be expected to create soon.

Once the topics are in place, it should be clear who needs to attend to the meeting. If possible, try to pick the minimum number of people who might need to attend, as duplicate decision coverage from key stakeholders tends to be inefficient.

Let the necessity of the project guide you to good meeting topics.

Putting so much thought into an agenda might seem like overkill. But remember, a meeting is a lot like what you eat: **what you get out of a meeting can only be as good as what you put in**.

Agenda Throwdown

Let's look at what makes agendas good and bad. Figure 3-1 presents an example of a well-thought-out agenda, while Figure 3-2 presents an example of what to avoid.

The good:

USC ASC NT
Beta Testing Kick-Off

AGENDA

Monday, May 17th, 2010, 2 – 3 PM
GoToMeeting (virtual)

Connection details

- Call into: (630) 869-1020; Access Code: 139-058-554
- Log into: https://www2.gotomeeting.com/join/139058554

Meeting goals: Provide training on the beta system to start a week of hands-on testing by the Annenberg/Neon Tommy team.

Agenda

1. Project status update
2. About beta testing
3. Submitting feedback
4. Getting help during testing
5. Logging into the site
6. System training (see outline)
7. Next steps

Participants:

- Wendy M. Chapman (USC)
- Marc Cooper (USC)
- Neon Tommy editorial team (USC)
- Justin Emond (UI)

Figure 3-1. An example of a well-organized agenda for the beta kickoff training for the editorial team of NeonTommy.com

The bad:

Agenda

1. What are our goals of the meeting?
2. How do our goals meet our internal goals?
3. Users
4. 3 reports
5. Data feed received

Figure 3-2. An unprofessional and unclear agenda

Why is the "good" agenda better?

- The bad agenda does not list a start and end time, so the **expectation of meeting length is not managed**. It will be harder to force the group to conclude the meeting and arrive at decisions in light of time pressure.
- The bad agenda **does not clearly state the goal** of the meeting. If you have not identified the meeting goal before the meeting starts, you will not have a strong premise to help you guide the discussion to resolving what you need resolved to move forward.
- The bad agenda is **unprofessional**, lacking an attendee list, a project or client identifier, and a location.
- Several agenda items on the bad agenda are not actionable, like "Users" and "3 reports." What is the goal of these items in the meeting? It cannot be to just talk about reports and users. You likely need to verify report formats and identify a user list or confirm user roles—but this is not clear.
- The bad agenda items **lack specificity**, which would help steer the discussion to the resolution you need to move forward.
- The bad agenda items lack parallel structure. Whenever possible, agenda items should be formatted the same way by, for example, starting each item with action verbs like identify, review, and verify.
- There is no final agenda item in the bad agenda to summarize **next steps**. A final "next steps" agenda item is helpful to conclude the

meeting with a brief summary of where things will move following the meeting.

Tip   A great agenda is specific, has clear goals, and includes actionable items.

You will notice a common theme among all of the criticisms here: maintaining momentum. Momentum in all phases of the project is crucial to keeping your efforts efficient and completing a project on schedule—two vital prerequisites to project success.

Running a Meeting

"If you don't know where you are going, any road will get you there," author Lewis Carroll famously wrote in *Alice's Adventures in Wonderland*. The same is true of running a project.

Most people who do not have experience running meetings tend to make a similar set of mistakes, which leads to unproductive meetings:

- They lose control of the meeting;
- They let the meeting run on too long; and
- They do not focus the discussion around the agenda.

The participants in your meeting want someone to assert control and run the meeting well. The participants want to be helpful and want to feel valued. If you run the meeting well and provide participants with a clear framework on how participants can contribute, the meeting will be successful, and the participants will thank you (sometimes, quite effusively) for running the meeting.

Take Charge

The key to running a successful meeting is to take charge. Taking charge of the meeting should happen early, even before the meeting begins.

And remember from the previous section, "Don't Waste Time: Write an Agenda," two important tips:

- You should know what outcome you want from the meeting.
- Take the time to prepare an agenda and distribute it to the participants several days before the meeting.

Tip Typically, participants will filter into the room, video, or conference call. To assert your control over the meeting, it is important that you make eye contact and welcome each participant.

Sometimes, meeting leaders will allow meetings to start late if key people have not yet arrived. Unless there is a specific reason to do so, avoid this approach. If you regularly start your meetings late, people will arrive increasingly late to your meetings. However, if all participants know that your meetings start on time, participants will arrive on time because they know that they will be embarrassed by walking in late or entering a telephone conference late.

Starting the Meeting

Today's meetings take place in a variety of formats: videoconference, webinar, telephone conference, in-person meetings, or a combination of formats. Regardless of the format, you can demonstrate your leadership by opening the meeting with a phrase like, "Let's get started. First of all, thank you all for taking time out of your busy schedules to participate in today's meeting." This simple statement establishes your control of the meeting but also recognizes the value of the participants' time.

As we have noted, most people do not like meetings. You can quickly win these skeptics over by recognizing that this meeting will only take as long as absolutely necessary. It is easy to do this with a statement like, "We have a full agenda, but I want to ensure that we respect your time today, so I will keep us moving along on the agenda to ensure that we conclude our meeting on time, or even a little early today."

Introduce the Agenda

Finally, so that people know where the meeting is headed, start by briefly reviewing the agenda. This can be as simple as stating the meeting goals and briefly reading through the three to five items on the agenda. When you have finished summarizing the agenda, you can ask simply, "Does this agenda sound appropriate, or does anyone recommend any modifications?" If there is an obvious senior or key leader in the room, this statement can be addressed directly to her.

Ninety-nine percent of the time, if you distributed the agenda several days prior to the meeting, no one will try to take over your meeting or change the agenda because they will know that this agenda has been planned for some time. In the unusual case where someone attempts to insert into the agenda an entirely irrelevant subject, you can suggest that the new item will be added to the agenda as a discussion point and then make a point of writing it down on your own agenda to make that person feel as if her recommendation has been heard. If it turns out that you do not have time to cover this new item during the meeting, recognize the item at the conclusion of the meeting by suggesting that you will add it as an agenda item to the next meeting.

If you have more than five items on your agenda, you should break the items into a series of shorter meetings, even if the meetings have to be conducted one after the other. The problem with having too many items on an agenda is that people tend to get bogged down on the early items, leaving you with little time to discuss the later items.

Guiding the Meeting

Once the meeting starts, you have three responsibilities:

- Ensure a smooth and consistent flow to the meeting. This can include introducing the background for an item on the agenda, and then asking the responsible person (if it is not you) to discuss the topic. At some point when the discussion around that item is complete, you can introduce the next item on the agenda.
- Track the action items. Each time there is a specific action (no matter how small) that is assigned, volunteered, or implied, write it down as a brief sentence, with the name of the person who will need to get it done.
- End the meeting on time.

As you complete each item on your agenda, wrap up that item by stating something like, "Great. Is there any further discussion on this item before we move onto the next item on our agenda?" This will emphasize to the participants that even though there has been much discussion from others, you remain in control and will continue to set the pace of the meeting. Knowing that you are still in control, even after a heated debate, puts many participants at ease.

The primary challenge to accomplishing your responsibilities in running the meeting, of course, is that participants get sidetracked and begin discussing an issue that is not related to the agenda. This is undoubtedly the hardest part of running a meeting and requires some finesse.

Here are several quick techniques to help get the meeting back on track:

- When a meeting participant is talking endlessly about a topic, you can politely interrupt when they take a breath, acknowledge that what they are discussing is important, and then state you will add it to the agenda for continued discussion at a later point. Then ask if there are any other comments about the active agenda item. This is admittedly hard to do, especially when the person you are inter-rupting is important. Sometimes, in the interest of politics, there simply is nothing to be done. In this case, you can try asking the par-ticipant a question that attempts to bring the topic back to the meeting at hand.

- When a meeting gets off track, you can quickly restore order by stating, "This is an important issue, but we won't be able to respect your time and resolve this issue during our meeting today. Let's put this item on the agenda for a future meeting or follow-up call, and get back to today's agenda." This technique shows that you are pushing the meeting back on track to respect the participants but, at the same time, identifying a time when the issue can be addressed. Participants in the meeting will love you for doing this.

- When you find that you have reached an impasse on an agenda item, and further discussion will not be productive, you can con-clude discussion with a phrase like, "It appears that we won't be able to resolve this issue during our meeting today. I've recorded where we are on this issue so we can come back to it at some fu-ture time. Let's proceed with the next item on the agenda."

Winding Down the Meeting

If your meeting is still under way and there are only 15 minutes remaining in the planned meeting time, let the participants know that the meeting needs to begin winding down: "We only have 15 minutes left for our meeting to-day. I want to respect your time and ensure that our meeting ends on time. Let's put the current discussion on our next meeting agenda, and move on to our final agenda item."

With only 7 minutes left, you need to wrap up the meeting. Typically, the last item on your agenda should be something like, "Review Action Items." You can signal the wrap-up of the meeting with a simple phrase like, "I want to respect your time and end our meeting on schedule, so we need to wrap up. Let me just summarize our action items."

At this point, you should summarize each of the action items you recorded during the meeting, and look at the person to whom each task is assigned. When you are done with your list, ask if there are any other action items you missed.

Finally, with a few minutes remaining, thank the participants for their time, and adjourn the meeting; "I want to thank each of you again for taking time out of what I know must be a very busy day to participate in our meeting. I will be following up via e-mail with the action items we identified during our meeting."

Meeting Wrap-Up

The key to a successful meeting is direction, momentum, and decisions. Really, these are all the same thing: ensure that the meeting moves the project from point A to B, no matter how small or large that might be. The key is **progress toward completing your project**. The goal of the meeting wrap-up is then the same: take the progress you made during the meeting and move forward.

The simplest way to move forward from a meeting is to identify the next steps, decisions, and deliverables needed from the project team in the form of action items. A *deliverable* is a document you provide to the client. An *action item* is simple: it's something you need someone to do. This is a **specific, individual, attainable task** that needs to be completed for the project to move forward.

This task could be work product (for example, identifying primary navigation items) or a decision (for example, deciding whether to use a fixed or fluid-width design).

An e-mail is a great format for a meeting wrap-up. Here are some tips:

- **Brevity** is important. Keep the e-mail and individual action items as short as possible.
- **Thank everyone** for taking the time to participate in the meeting.
- Identify and **list each action item** identified in the meeting.

- **Label each item with initials** to clearly name the person who is responsible for completing that item. (Items assigned to a group or to no one will never be completed because no one is responsible for them.)
- Clearly **identify the next steps** from the meeting (commonly an updated document following feedback, some other kind of deliverable, or the decision to proceed with the next phase of the project).

Your Monday morning checklist (see Chapter 6) is a great time to review any meeting follow-up e-mails you sent out in the previous week and "ping" people on tasks assigned to them to prod some work product out of your client. You can forward the meeting follow-up e-mail from your Sent folder with a short note that says something like this:

> Hi {client first name},
>
> I just wanted to check in on the {action items}.
>
> If there is anything I can do to help, please don't hesitate to let me know.
>
> Thanks,
> {call sign}

A quick e-mail like this is a polite way to guilt the client into action on the task they promised to complete. **A little guilt can go a long way**. Some people may regard the forwarding of an unanswered e-mail to be aggressive. However, if you wait a reasonable amount of a time for a reply (3 business days) and do not receive one, then the recipient may feel too guilty about not replying to feel overly managed.

Tip If you use a project management tool (see the Appendix for a list of tools), action items are perfectly suited to become tasks that you can assign to project and client team members.

What About Minutes?

Frequently, the act of taking or sending meeting minutes is rather pointless. In most cases, the only notes that ought to be taken during a meeting are action items, because action items represent decisions and progress toward project completion that are discussed during the meeting.

Meetings are not about remembering discussion (that is what minutes are great for), they are about deciding action. This is why action items are useful because they are specific, individual, attainable tasks that move the project toward completion.

Wrap-Up E-mail Example

Here is a sample e-mail that summarizes a meeting where the client reviewed the first draft of wireframes we prepared.

> Hi Team,
>
> Thanks for taking the time today to chat about the draft wireframes for the new {project name} web site. I collected great feedback during our call.
>
> Here are the action items I collected during our meeting:
>
> 1. Confirm primary navigation items (Wendy)
>
> 2. Provide three example images from existing site (Wendy)
>
> 3. Research options for using Flash in the navigation (Justin)
>
> 4. Determine fixed vs. fluid width (Gabe)
>
> 5. Prepare a set of refined wireframes (Justin)
>
> 6. Approve updated wireframes (Wendy)
>
> I'll take all of the comments I collected today and prepare a new set of wireframes. I expect to have to the updated wireframes to you by the end of next week.
>
> If there is anything else you need or if you have any questions, kindly let me know.
>
> Thanks,
> {call sign}

Wrapping Up

Hopefully by this point you have a good sense of how disastrous to the health of the project Greg's approach to meetings is. It is no surprise his project was put on hold by the client. He didn't plan ahead, didn't take control of the meeting, and didn't build confidence with his client.

Preparing agendas and paying attention to the clock sound pretty dry, but a well-executed, well-planned meeting can keep the project running smoothly and everyone involved happy.

Meetings are especially vital during the first real phase of the project when you conduct discovery. It is during discovery that you clearly define exactly what the project will entail. What you define in discovery defines what you do for the rest of the project lifecycle. In Chapter 4, we go into detail on how to manage this crucial phase.

Discovery and Requirements

By now you should have a signed scope of work with the client and be ready to actually start the project. Where to begin? That's easy: discovery. Discovery is a vital first step in your project. In discovery, you turn the vague feature outlines in the proposal into detailed, actionable lists of features that will be built.

Discovery is vital for a variety of reasons, so we start with a clear explanation of why we think it's so important. We then look at the two main kinds of documents that get created in this phase: sitemaps and requirements documents. We show you how to gather requirements, how to format the document, and some guiding principles on what makes a good requirement.

To wrap up, we also cover the importance of getting the client to approve the requirements for the project and dealing with out-of-scope requests (a challenge on almost any project).

Why Discovery?

Discovery is the process by which you identify exactly what you and your team are going to build.

The goal of the discovery phase is to help manage the client's expectations by making it very clear what exact features the project will contain. The first document in a project is usually the scope of work (see Chapter 2). The scope of work is nebulous by design; you do not have time at this phase of the project to invest in identifying all of the requirements of the system, and it is not necessary to have this precise list to create a proposed project budget.

Consider the difference between the scope of work and discovery as "what" vs. "how." The scope of work might include, "Develop a web interface for importing contact records in an external file." That's the "what." The discovery process gets into details—the "how." How the file will be formatted, with what frequency will the file be imported, and what should happen when errors are encountered.

For the project to be successful, it must be crystal clear to the project manager—and thus the project team—and the client exactly what the system will do. For example, in a scope of work, the sentence, "The web site will contain a blog," can mean one thing to a client and an entirely different thing to a project manager. The client might envision a blog that allows users to create podcast posts that integrate with iTunes automatically and include a one-click method to embed uploaded video, while the project manager might simply picture a blog limited to user posts with a title, body, and date of publication, and nothing else. The whole point of discovery is to ask questions like, "What do you need the blog to do?"

Identifying the requirements for a project will help reveal any disconnect between the client's expectations and yours. It is in this phase when those **disparities will appear and when they can be addressed at the lowest cost**. (For handling out-of-scope requirements, see "Dealing with Out-of-Scope Requirements" later in this chapter.)

Discovery is a clear critical path item. You absolutely should not proceed with design or development until you have a discovery document finalized and approved by the client.

Depending on the project type, there are two kinds of documents you can create to complete project discovery. For a **web site redesign project, a sitemap is sufficient**. A web site redesign tends to focus less on custom application development and the features that come with it and more on capturing the configuration of the new version of a public web site. A public web site has a set number of ways that it tends to behave, while an application is an entirely customized experience.

For custom application development, then, a more robust process is in order: the requirements document. Read on for more about sitemaps and requirements documents.

The Sitemap Document

A sitemap document is typically a large checklist of questions separated into logical sections that cover all of the decision points in creating a web site.

The components that make up a modern, standards-driven web site are common, so you can keep a sitemap template document for use when starting a new project. Some questions in our sitemap template are mundane, some are obvious, and some are deliberately qualitative.

Typically, our sitemap document has the following sections:

- **Web site purpose**: Explicitly covers simple details like the official name of the web site, the URL, and primary goals with redesigning the web site
- **Features**: Identifies the precise components of the web site (like e-mail newsletter integration and social icons)
- **Design brief**: Captures nebulous client thoughts on how the design should look
- **Information architecture**: Identifies page-level features such as navigation, home page components, and footer
- **Technical brief**: Identifies the technology stack that will be used to power the site

Example Questions

Here are some questions from our sitemap template:

- What is the official name of the web site?
- What are the business and marketing objectives of the project (for example, to increase membership, promote content, increase sales)?
- Who are the primary audiences? Identify a few unique characteristics about each audience.
- How many non-HTML document files of what type will be included on the site (.pdf, .doc, .xls, etc.)?
- Will the navigation system include breadcrumbs?
- Will there be a signup feature?
- Please select three to five designs that you like and describe what you like about them.

- Please identify by name and URL the web sites of three competitors, and identify what you like or dislike about these web sites.
- Use at least three adjectives to describe the overall feeling or perception the web site should convey. (Examples: conservative, green, progressive, friendly, formal, casual, professional, energetic, etc.)
- What colors do you prefer? What colors should not be used?
- What are the additional branding or content elements that should appear on the home page?
- What are the top-level navigation categories that will appear on every page?
- Should navigation appear horizontally across the top or vertically down the left side?
- What content management system will be used?
- How many web site authors will be updating the web site? (Identify by name.)
- What are the various administrative functions, and what level of authority will each function need? What will be the process for developing content, submitting content, and approving content before it is published?
- What are the various types of content (news, events, newsletters, reports, etc.) on the web site?
- How should your content be organized? (Geography, topic, etc.)
- Who is your domain registrar, and who has the username/password?
- Will the web site include video or audio? How should this content be delivered?
- Are any additional security precautions warranted?

Sitemap Workflow

Prior to the initial project kickoff meeting, you should be able to make a first pass at the sitemap workflow document and fill in everything that you know already about the client or can identify from the existing site. What you fill in on this first draft will allow you to frame the discussion of the questions raised in this document. A first pass also allows you to identify any potential complications that might arise from the client's goals of the web site and give you time to mitigate them in your draft answers.

A completed draft pass on this document can serve as the main task of your project kickoff meeting. You can share this draft prior to the meeting and spend the time in the meeting reviewing each proposed answer and addressing questions that were not possible to answer on your first pass. The discussion that ensues in obtaining these answers will be illustrative and should foster any major missing features or goals from the client. Additionally, the goal is clear in such a meeting: obtain answers to every question in the document.

Following the meeting review of this document, you should be able to produce a near-final version for circulation and review by the team. Typically, you would produce one or two additional minor revisions of the document following the major review meeting and the major second version. Most importantly, be clear when you first e-mail the document for review that the project cannot proceed until this version is approved by the client.

About Requirements

For a web application development project, a requirements document is a more suitable discovery document than a site map for cataloging features.

A **requirement is a specific and concise summary of a feature** that the project must contain. Here are some examples from real requirements documents we have prepared:

- System will track campaign name and up to a 12-campaign touchstep sequence Next action date will be calculated by adding in the days after value for the next unapplied step in the campaign sequence to the current date
- System will allow search results to be exported to CSV format, which will include the same fields as the search
- System will include a screen to upload specifically formatted lists of prospects into the system
- System will run on server-class hardware
- System interface will run inside of a web browser (Microsoft Internet Explorer version 7 or above or Mozilla Firefox version 2 or above)

The requirements document turns into a great checklist that the project manager can use to easily verify task completion from the developers on the project. The individual requirements on a printed copy of the requirements document can be ticked off as progress is made throughout the entire project to track progress and completion.

Tip Be careful: you don't need to document everything. A requirement that has no alternative or is redundant to another requirement probably doesn't need much clarifying.

The requirements document also serves as a reference during discussions in later phases of the project **to protect against scope creep**. If the requirements are clearly laid out at the start of the project, then the project manager can more easily determine (and explain to the client) if new requests fall inside or outside of the scope of the project.

Here are some common requirements that tend to appear in projects:

- User accounts and roles (How many and how granular?)
- System or audit logging
- Settings screens for drop-down menus and lookup tables
- Server hardware, security, and backup requirements (for clients that will provide their own hardware for the application)
- Record search and filter controls
- Data import utility
- E-mail integration (Will the system send e-mail? Will the system export e-mail lists to an external newsletter system?)
- Specifics on the technology stack (What database software is needed? Reporting software? Backups?)
- Bulk editing
- Duplicate data or record management

How to Gather Requirements for Fun and Profit

The best ways to gather the requirements of a project are to—*wait for it*— hold a requirements gathering meeting. Prepare an agenda for the meeting in which the items to be addressed are the major sections of the project as identified in the scope of work.

In general, the goal of the project kickoff meeting should be to

- Introduce your process;
- Identify or confirm the key project goals, requirements, and risks; and
- Identify future meetings that will need to be conducted on specific topics.

In most cases, we find it useful to prepare a draft discovery and requirements questionnaire for the kickoff meeting. This document organizes questions about the project in logical categories that will correspond to the agenda. For example, if we were discussing the visual design, we would ask questions such as

- What do you like about your current web site?
- What are three web sites that represent the visual look you seek?
- What logo and branding identity requirements does your organization have?
- For what size interface should the design be optimized?

Here are a few additional questions that are common to ask in requirements gathering meetings:

- How many users are there?
- How many user roles?
- What user actions should be audited?
- What are the primary web site navigation items?

Having all these questions in one place makes us feel more comfortable about the meeting because there is less to remember. It also makes it easy for us to record notes during the meeting, and it helps the client stay on track.

We like to distribute the draft document prior to the meeting so that everyone knows what we will cover. However, different project managers have different styles; some prefer to keep this document as a personal reference.

The key to the requirements document meeting is to touch upon every part of the project scope and ask questions until you feel confident that you understand what the client expects each piece to do.

Tip Think of it this way: you are building the specific module or feature in question, and you are going through the process of putting the feature set together with whatever tools will be used. In doing this, you will occasionally come across implementation gaps where it is not clear how a piece should work. This is a great question to then immediately raise with the client.

You will have to turn the notes you take during this meeting into the requirements document.

TAKING NOTES

Justin was never taught how to take notes in high school. Consequently, when he started college, he used the same note-taking strategy that worked well in high school: write everything down. Although this was manageable in high school, where teachers meander from topic to topic, it was downright painful in college. There is simply too much information to write down in the compressed class times, because they usually met only twice per week.

One day, as he sat with a cramped hand in class struggling to keep up, a thought occurred to him: why not only write down what I will need later (read: the final exam)? It is a simple but powerful thought: do not take notes for the sake of notes; instead, have a clear goal in mind about why you are taking notes, and let that goal guide your approach.

The same tip applies for a meeting: **have a clear goal in mind for what you need to do after the meeting, and take notes accordingly**. If this is a requirements gathering meeting, then your post-meeting goal is clear: write the requirements document.

This style of note taking has another benefit: you will likely think of other questions that have not been answered. This is the perfect time to ask those questions and get clarification.

When it comes time to turn your notes into the requirements document, you are ahead of the game because you already have the core requirements right there, in your notes.

Tip While in the meeting, try to imagine that you are writing the requirements document at that very moment. Do you need notes on every detail of what was discussed? No, you simply need to jot down requirements as you hear them, in the same format you will use when preparing the actual document.

The Requirements Document Structure

At this point, you have—hopefully—had a good requirements gathering meeting and have a sense of what the project needs to do. If you took good notes in earlier meetings, then writing the actual requirements document should be easy.

Here are a few general tips for the **requirements document format**:

- Make this a formal client document. Include a **title page** with your logo, author name, name of the project, client name, preparation date, version number, and filename.
- **Split the document** into major sections covering the major modules of the project.
- Use a clear file naming convention, like "20110924-client-code-requirements-document-v1" (the "v" stands for version number and should be incremented each time the document is sent to the client).
- Assign each requirement a **unique identifier**. The easiest way to do this is to use your text editor's built-in number list tool.
- Modify the **number format of your requirements** to be R#.#, where the first number is automatically the section number and the second number is the item number. Examples: R2.13, 8.3 and 11.12.
- Start the requirements by copying a previous document. You will end up discarding most of the old document, but you can preserve the document fidelity, layout, style, and numbering format (which are a pain to set up the first time around in Microsoft Word).

Requirements should be concise and specific. This way, the requirements document protects both you and the client: the document manages the client's expectations, reduces the chance of misunderstandings, and protects you throughout the project against scope creep. Figure 4-1 presents an excerpt from a requirements document from one of our projects.

USC ASC - CMS Drupal Development Requirements Document

R3.27	When listed, stories will include taxonomy/section(s), the title, author(s), publish date and teaser.	n/a
R3.28	System will allow a user to split a story into a set number of pages.	✓ Medium
R3.29	System will allow users to select display format for each individual story detail page.	✓ Medium
R3.30	System will include up to three story detail page layouts. Annenberg team will identify layouts before development.	✓ Medium
R3.31	Story detail page will show taxonomy/section(s), story title, story body, rich media (see next section), free tags, author, author title, publish date, side bar story, trackback count, comment count and a comments form.	n/a
R3.32	System story details page will include a series of links to "Share it" with up to 10 sites, including Digg, Facebook, Twitter, Delicious, LinkedIn and StumbleUpon.	n/a
R3.33	Story detail page will include a block to show the top 10 most recent related stories by taxonomy.	n/a
R3.34	Story detail page will include a block to show the top 10 most read stories of all time.	n/a
R3.35	System will automatically capture new revisions when nodes are updated.	n/a
R3.36	System will store all revisions for nodes.	n/a
R3.37	System will allow users to rollback nodes to previous revisions.	n/a
R3.38	System will allow users to compare nodes to previous revisions.	n/a
R3.39	System will automatically post to a single Twitter account on new story creation.	n/a
R3.40	System will automatically post a status update to a single Facebook user profile on new story creation.	✓ Low
R3.41	System will allow users to post to an individual user blog.	n/a
R3.42	System will allow users to create blogs posts with rich media (see below).	n/a

4. FUNCTIONAL REQUIREMENTS – RICH MEDIA

Reqmt ID	Description	Custom Dev
R4.1	System will support attaching rich media components to story nodes.	n/a
R4.2	System will include a rich text editor, for using complex formatting in the creation of body text.	n/a
R4.3	System will include the following complex editing functions: bold, italics, underline, strike-through, bullets, numbered lists, indents, block quotes, images, links, tables and anchors.	n/a
R4.4	System will allow users to attach video, audio and images to story nodes as file attachments.	n/a

Figure 4-1. An excerpt from a requirements document for NeonTommy.com

Requirements-Writing Principles

We've identified five requirements-writing principles and created examples that demonstrate those principles. In this section, we'll walk through these principles, and conclude with some additional tips for completing the requirements document.

Principle #1: Protect the Scope of the Project

Example requirement: System will track up to 25 user profile fields, including first name, middle name, last name, e-mail address, phone number, title, and short note.

This example demonstrates two important concepts:

- Be as **specific as possible where imagination can run free**. The client might imagine tracking 150 fields for a user profile, thinking that the system is a customer relationship management tool, where you might imagine a few simple fields.
- Protect the scope of the project. You might not know all of the profile fields the system will track at the time of writing of this document, and that is fine. Include the fields you have identified, and set an upper boundary that limits how far this feature can be taken.

Principle #2: Mention Every Settings Screen

Example requirement: System will include a screen to add and modify to the standard list of prospect sources.

If a drop-down menu, lookup table, or other value used in the system will be managed in a settings screen accessible to the user, mention it. Make it clear what kinds of settings the user will be able to edit and what kinds are built into the system.

Principle #3: Mention the Audit Logging

Example requirement: System will include a system log to track major system events (such as file imports and duplicate merges).

If the system includes any kind of audit logging (that is, logging of events that happen in the system), specify it in the requirements document.

Principle #4: Be Clear What the Search Will and Will Not Do

Example requirement: System will enable users to enter multiple ZIP codes for a filter.

In this example, we specify that the ZIP code field will allow a user to enter in multiple ZIP codes to perform an OR search on multiple locations.

Search is a big, hard, complex problem. If your application will include a search tool, be very specific on how the search will work, what kinds of advanced search options are possible, and exactly how queries will work.

When you say *search* to the client, you might think of a simple screen with two filter fields, but the client might want something like the advanced query screen in their e-mail client. The client will have his own conception of what search is. Make it clear.

Principle #5: Specify the Compatible Browsers

Example: System interface will run inside of a web browser (Microsoft Internet Explorer version 7 or above or Mozilla Firefox version 2 or above).

There are three major operating systems (Windows, Linux, and Mac OS X) and more than six major browsers with various levels of compatibility across each platform. Although it is likely that your project will work well in most browsers, it is important to specify up front what platforms will have your focus. This will also help reveal at the start of the project if the client's desktop technology is not what you are assuming.

Here are some additional tips for writing the requirements document:

- Take a few moments to **visualize the application** in your head, and specifically the screens that you can imagine the application will have. Is there anything you are missing? Imagine you are working on those screens. Is there anything missing you might need?
- **Ambiguity will haunt you later**. Throughout the process of writing the requirements document, there will inevitably be decisions that have yet to be made and open issues to resolve. You will be tempted to leave these unanswered. Don't. When you leave something unspecified, it will rear its ugly head at the least opportune moment.

- If you have a lengthy piece of information—like a data import schema—add this as an appendix to the document and reference the appendix in the appropriate requirement.
- It is likely that you will go through several iterations of the requirements document during this process of preparation and client review. For ease of review, consider **underlining the requirements that you add or change on the version 2 or later** copies of the document. This will make it very clear to the client exactly what changed and exactly what she needs to review.
- Do not fret! Once you have written several of these documents, you will already know what 25%-30% of the requirements need to be without the need for notes. They will get easier to write over time.

The 80/20 Rule

In 1906, an economist named Vilfredo Pareto noticed that 80% of the land in his native Italy was owned by 20% of the population. When he looked at land ownership in other countries, he found the same ratio. In the United States, 20% of the population uses about 80% of the health care resources. Microsoft noted that by fixing 20% of the bugs in Windows they could fix 80% of the crashes.

What all of these figures have in common is that these ratios break at the 80/20 divide. Generally speaking, 80% of your issue is caused by 20% of your population—be that elite land owners, bugs, or sick people. This 80/20 rule appears in other disciplines, like computer science and electrical engineering, where you often solve most (80%) of your performance problems by looking at the least optimum part (20%).

The principle to apply to project management relates specifically to requirements gathering. No matter how feature-rich, no customized or out-of-the-box solution will ever serve 100% of your client's requirements. Some requirements will contradict others on the way to 100% coverage; some will be more time-consuming than entire modules of your project. Abraham Lincoln famously said that you cannot please all the people all the time. This is true in project management, too. **You cannot meet all the requirements all the time**.

The lesson from the 80/20 rule in project management, then, is to focus on meeting 80% of the client's requirements and letting the client understand the cost and effort implication of the other 20%. That way, the client can decide if the effort required for implementing this additional 20% is worth the budget. Trying to build or find a solution to meet near 100% of client requirements will make the project dramatically more expensive (either for the client if properly budgeted or for you if not) and very long. By focusing on the major requirements and features that best serve the overall goals of the project, you reduce the cost to the client and reduce the risk to the project itself.

But more importantly, it is that 80% or so of requirements that the client probably really needs. There are always things a client might request that are unnecessary or really unhelpful to their workflow. This ratio will never be perfectly 80/20, but there will always be some additional requirements that, given some perspective, do not add value to the project or benefit your client.

Getting the Requirements Approved

Once the document is complete, you can send a draft to the client for review and, if needed, set up another call with the client to go over their feedback and answer any questions. If you have an active client who takes the time to really read the document, this call will likely yield some great questions relating to how their workflow will fit into the new system. The needed refinements to the requirements document will be easy to make.

More often than not, however, getting the client to actually review a document—instead of just glancing at the e-mail with the attachment—can be a challenge.

The best way to force your client to review the document is to state very clearly that they must sign off on the requirements document before the project can continue.

Here are a few tips:

- As a first step, send the first version of the **client-ready requirements document** but call it a draft. This sets the tone for the client to know they can suggest changes.
- Set up a meeting to review the first draft of the requirements document. This should force them to review the document before the meeting.
- In the meeting, identify any missing requirements.

- Add in the missing requirements, send the updated draft to the client, and ask them pointedly if this is ready for approval. Gently remind them that the project cannot proceed until they sign off on the document.

Be sure to resist any requests from the client to proceed with development before the requirements document is approved. Should you proceed, you will lose any leverage you have to get the document accepted formally. The client will respect your polite but stern insistence that approval is a critical step before proceeding further.

Dealing with Out-of-Scope Requirements

When preparing a requirements document, be sure to collect all the requirements the client articulates, not just the requirements that you deem to be in scope. When you prepare the requirements document, you will be able to identify the requirements that are out of scope in the document. This approach helps the client understand that that not everything they requested is part of the scope—and budget. This approach also helps set the client's expectations that future requests will need to be evaluated and budgeted and that your development effort is not an unlimited resource.

Tip When you identify just one or two items that are out of scope, there is a temptation to just include these items in the project so you do not disappoint your client. As you collect a larger number of out-of-scope requirements, however, it becomes more obvious that the large number of out-of-scope items quickly accumulates into a significant effort.

Wrapping Up

By now you should (hopefully) have a good grasp of the importance of discovery and be ready to accurately detail all of the intended functionality of your project. By conducting a strong discovery phase, you position your project well for every later phase of the life cycle. Well-managed expectations and well-managed detail at this phase will protect your project budget and your sanity.

Broadly speaking, when you complete discovery, you proceed with development. This is likely to be the longest phase of your project, using the most project hours. Additionally, once you complete requirements gathering, you should be able to schedule out the remainder of the project with confidence. With this in mind, in the next chapter we look at all of the ins and outs of scheduling and budgeting your project.

We talk about estimating time (never an easy task), how to keep a close eye on things without making your team feel micromanaged, and more details on dealing with the inevitable out-of-scope requests that come in from the client.

Project Schedule and Budgeting

Oh, the Horror of Just One More Delay

Mary is a public relations manager for a nonprofit agency. She is charged with redesigning the organization's web site and integrating it with a new financial system the organization is implementing. Although Mary does not have any experience with web site development, she is a regular user of e-mail and sometimes reads popular news web sites and makes online purchases. Mary writes down all the things she wants the new web site to do and then asks her friends for recommendations for consultants and firms. Over the next several months, she gets ten different proposals, from 2 pages to more than 50 pages, ranging from a few hundred dollars to over $30,000. With such a wide range of proposals, Mary takes nearly a month to select the two firms that she likes best and schedules interviews with them. Although the proposals are very different and seem to propose different technologies, Mary selects the firm that seems to do the most work with nonprofits and signs the contract for services.

Mary needs to move fast because she had only budgeted 2 weeks to select a proposal and 2 months to develop the web site in order to meet the deadline she was given by her boss. She schedules the kickoff meeting the same day the contract is signed.

The day of the kickoff meeting, Mary's boss, Susan, is called away to handle an emergency and cannot participate in the meeting. The development manager is not interested in the project and will not participate either. Only the

CFO of the nonprofit is able to attend. The kickoff meeting goes very well, but toward the end of the meeting, it becomes clear that the CFO has not yet approved the project budget and has some problems with the contract Mary signed.

The consulting firm is ready to get started on the project, but Mary asks them to hold off while the nonprofit updates the contract and secures the funds. Mary and the CFO decide to review all of the proposals a second time and then rewrite the contract for the firm they selected. The new contract includes some requirements that were not part of the nonprofit's request for proposal (RFP) or the consulting firm's. Consequently, the consulting firm provides a change order for the additional work.

Finally, 3 months after the kickoff meeting, the project is ready to move forward, and Mary asks the consulting firm to prepare the designs in just a week. The consulting firm moves quickly. In just a few weeks it completes three rounds of design and Mary approves the final version. Development begins, but after a week, the nonprofit's CEO sees the designs for the first time. She halts the project while she revisits the designs.

Seeing the designs makes the CEO realize that she really needs to proceed with that rebranding effort that had been on hold for over a year, including a new logo and corporate color scheme. Mary is put in charge of writing an RFP to hire a branding firm to come up with the logo. The consulting firm is asked to put the project on hold for a month while the nonprofit goes through a rebranding effort. One month stretches into two, then three.

Fast-forward six months. It is now over a year since the project began. While the project is now 75% over budget, development of the web site based on a new set of designs is complete. The CEO and CTO are frustrated with the web site consulting firm and the branding firm because they believe both projects have taken far too long and both are over budget.

Protecting the schedule to avoid these situations is vital to project success. This chapter offers guidance on preparing a practical schedule and budget that enable you to stay on track and track your progress.

Estimating Time (It's Hard!)

One of the most critical tasks a project manager will undertake is estimating budgets. This is critical because task estimation will set the project scope, define the resources that need to be allocated for the project, and impact the proposed project schedule.

Because estimating is a hard task and is as much art as science, task estimation has a bit of a bad reputation. But fear not, intrepid reader, for you need not be so leery. Here are some tips to make estimating easier.

Principle #1: Account for Unknowns

It is impossible to accurately predict everything that might happen during a project task. There is always going to be the chance for an unexpected event to increase the time needed for a task. Consider adding a small amount of time on top of your estimate to account for this.

Principle #2: Break the Task into Parts

When thinking about a task for a project, break it down into pieces. Do not estimate the whole, just the parts. For example, say you are estimating the Drupal theming task for a modest web site (Drupal is a content management system). You might break this task down into splicing up the mock-up from the designer, creating the CSS and HTML, setting up the template files, and programming the views and blocks.

Principle #3: A Task is More Than Development

This idea might seem simple, but it is worth mentioning: the time to complete a task is only partly developer time. Do not forget about additional time for quality assurance (QA), meetings with the developer to discuss the technical specification, time to collect feedback from the client or internal stakeholders, and time to deploy the project to a staging server (and, if relevant, a production server).

Principle #4: Ask a Developer (But Add Time)

If you are estimating a task that you have not actually done in your past work life, stop. Find a developer in the office, provide a simple summary of the task (describe the task generically, but do mention any parts of the task that you consider to be challenging, difficult, or nonstandard work), and ask them how long it would take.

Now, take their estimate and add 50%, along with their developer bias (see Principle #5).

Wait, why should you add 50%? Because a developer is likely to estimate how long it will take them to sit down and knock the task out. They do not tend to think about the several rounds of refinements they are likely to do, nor do they think to include general project management and quality assurance time for a task. All of the time spent beyond what they do is likely to be a mystery to them, and so it simply will not appear in the estimate.

Principle #5: Know Your Bias (or, Review Your Actuals)

Providing good estimates for projects is an ongoing learning experience. It is important to take a moment at the end of a project phase, or at the end of a project, and check how long a task actually took. Compare the **actual** time the task took to complete with your original estimate. A pattern—or bias—will quickly emerge. You will likely be consistently incorrect in one manner or another, be that too high or, more typically, too low in your estimates.

Once you start to see your bias, be proactive and adjust your initial estimate by enough to counteract it. For example, if you think a task is going to take 3 days, and you typically underestimate by 50%, then estimate the task as 6 days.

Principle #6: Use Software to Help Report on Your Estimation Performance

There are many different project management software vendors. Several of them (see the Appendix) include reports that can detail the estimation accuracy history of individual team members. This makes it easy to track real-time data on estimation bias, which will help improve your estimates.

Principle #7: Resist the Temptation to Underestimate

There are many reasons why a project manager might feel pressure to compress an estimate. This pressure could come from a client with a restricted budget or a superior unwilling to allocate resources sufficient to complete the project.

Resist this temptation. Compressed estimates greatly risk project success and client happiness. **A task takes a set time to complete. It does not take less or more; it takes the time it takes.** Having a tighter budget means that the project manager will feel pressured to complete the task in less time. This pressure gets passed to the developer. Nobody likes to work under this kind of pressure.

An underestimated task will deliver pain to either the client or your superiors: if you complete the task to spec, the client will be happy but your project will be over budget. If you cut corners, the client will be (justifiably) unhappy.

Insist that if less time has to be spent on a task, then features have to be removed from the task requirements. Reducing the time spent should reduce the scope accordingly. This way, you can complete the task on budget and meet the expectations of the client.

Tip Meeting lowered expectations is far better for your relationship with your client than failing to meet greater expectations.

Preparing the Project Schedule

The goal of the project schedule is to set the project delivery expectations with the client. A good schedule has two components: a reasonable estimate for project completion and clearly identified milestones for critical deliverables.

Creating a project schedule is another frustrating part of project management that is based in estimates (read: guesses). Although it becomes easier to write schedules as you learn how long similar phases tend to take in other projects, here are some pointers that can help you write the schedule.

Principle #1: Identify Each Major Phase (but Be Concise)

Schedules should be simple to read, painless to update, and easy to e-mail. You do not need every minor project phase on a schedule. You do not need a giant ugly GANNT chart (they might seem like essential project management tools, but they really might only be applicable to projects larger than those we discuss here). You are not building a building; you are building a web site.

For a typical two- to three-month project with a budget of around $55,000, a ten-item schedule will be fine. For a four- to five-month project with a budget of $100,000 or more, you should have a project timeline with specificity and deliverables week-by-week.

Principle #2: Identify Critical Deliverables

A project schedule is most helpful to you when it can be used to clearly **demonstrate to the client where delays can occur and who is responsible for critical deliverables**. Make these clear on the first draft of the schedule and point them out to the client when you review the schedule together.

For example: if you have a project where the client is providing their own design, then you should have a step on your schedule that clearly states when the design must be completed, approved, signed, sealed, and delivered. When that date arrives—and passes—it will be very simple to alert the client that the project schedule is delayed.

We often label a critical deliverable "Critical Pathway," so a schedule item of "Provide logo and branding guidelines" becomes "Critical Pathway: Provide logo and branding guidelines."

Principle #3: Add Some Padding

There will be a delay in the project on your end. Something will go wrong. Just accept it. Maybe a team member will leave, or there will be a death in the family of a developer who will need time off, or maybe a high-profile support project will implode, requiring lots of unexpected attention to fix. Another project could appear that upper management deems higher priority.

The lesson is here is to embrace an old adage: assume the best, plan for the worst. Add some padding to the schedule.

Tip An estimate from a developer is probably off by 50%-100%. Why? Two reasons. First, programmers are eternal optimists, and second, estimates tend only to include the time for that first, great working draft of a module. They do not include time for testing, refinement, adjustments, art reviews, and so forth.

Principle #4: Learn Your Team's Bias

Because you rely so heavily on the estimates of your team (as their smaller estimates trickle up into your own larger estimates), it's vital to take an active role in learning and helping to improve their ability to make accurate estimates.

Principle #5: Alert the Client to Deadlines

If a critical deadline for a project deliverable is approaching, send a short, polite reminder to "check in on the status." Some project management tools (see the Appendix) do this for you automatically.

Principle #6: Include the Client's Critical Path Deadlines

Call out any key delivery dates that the client has identified clearly, which may or may not be project-specific.

Formatting the Schedule

If you use a project management tool (see the Appendix), the schedule is likely to be provided for you in a clean and professional manner. In these cases, assuming your clients have accounts, you can simply send a link to your client to access the schedule in that tool for review and discussion.

If you are preparing a schedule manually and want to send it to the client, you will need to format it yourself. A simple schedule of around 12 to 15 items can be presented cleanly in an e-mail. Anything longer would look better in a software tool. For example:

Hi Team,

I've prepared a draft project schedule for the development of the web site.

Kindly take a look and let me know if you have any questions, changes, or concerns. I would be happy to setup a conference call to discuss further if you like.

Draft Project Schedule

===================

4/1: Project schedule and requirements document ready

4/10: Server specs provided

4/10: Critical Pathway: Provide style guide, logo

4/15: Critical Pathway: Approve requirements document

5/5: Design Mock-up Ready

5/12: Critical Pathway: Design feedback

5/20: Critical Pathway: Provide existing content

5/20: Critical pathway: Provide GAC photos

5/20: Critical Pathway: Design approved

5/20: Critical Pathway: Server hardware, SSL cert ready

6/20: Content migration complete

6/25: Site ready for ICANN review

6/30: Drupal training, part 1

6/31: Drupal training, part 2

7/15: Site ready for launch

Cheers,

{call sign}

Keeping a Close Eye on the Project (without Micromanaging)

Maybe, like us, you have had the experience of trying to straighten up a closet and getting distracted. While you are organizing a shelf, you discover that box of networking cables you had been meaning to sort through. Then you come across that broken webcam and you remember you now have the missing part, and start to fix it, but you cannot find the cable. Then you discover another box with cables that need to be sorted and cleaned out. . . Before long, you are 2 hours into a task on which you had planned to spend only 10 minutes.

Development can be like this. Even really great developers can get distracted with tangential work. What started out as a 1-day project can quickly explode into a weeklong project if not planned and managed well.

An example: a project manager asks a developer to participate in a meeting with several other team members to discuss a new client project that needs to be scoped out—a web application optimized for delivery on mobile devices. During the meeting, the team decides to look around at the existing products to see if one might be a good fit. The project manager asks a developer to check out three products that might provide a good starting point for the mobile application. The project manager thinks this is a 1- to 2-hour task. The developer thinks that this sounds like great fun. Three days later, the project manager checks in with the developer and finds that the developer has put 16 hours into evaluating, downloading, installing, and prototyping each of the tools. Now, the project is 2 days over budget before it has even been officially approved.

Most developers like technology, and many good developers are good at what they do because they like to push the boundaries and discover new applications and new approaches to solving problems.

Your challenge as a project manager is to guide this creative energy to ensure that it remains productive for your client. So how do you do this? No one—especially a developer—likes to be micromanaged.

You need to be able to keep developers on task and on schedule without having the appearance of looking over the developer's shoulder. Here are some techniques for managing a developer's time without making it look like you are sitting behind them while they code.

- **Check in**: Ask the developer to check in with you after spending X hours on the project, regardless of where they are with the project. This request is explicit and will provide you with a way to ensure that the he is heading in the right direction. For example, "check in with me after you have spent 4 hours on this task so we can review your code and the approach you have selected." If the developer is on the right track, create the next check-in for 8 hours, and so on. If the developer is not headed in the right direction, create the next check-in for 2 hours so you can confirm that he is back on track. Consider having developers revalidate (or adjust) their estimates when you check in. Eventually, most developers will begin to feel bad when it is clear that their poor estimates are responsible for a large percentage of slippage. Recognizing the problem is the first step toward dealing with it.
- **Milestones**: Chunk the task into a series of discrete milestones. Have each milestone be a 4- to 8-hour task. After each milestone, have the developer check back with you so you can evaluate his progress and provide feedback. As the project gets further along and you have more confidence in the direction he is taking, increase the size of the milestones. For example, if you are building a web application, have the developer implement a single screen that will display data from your data source.
- **Peer review**: If you do not have the technical expertise to be confident the developer is headed in the right direction, recruit a more senior developer you trust, and set up a peer-to-peer review. In some cases, you may prefer not to be in these meetings so that your senior developer can give the project developer feedback without having the developer feel like he is not performing. Peer reviews are also a great tool to help developers learn and improve. If you have a new project, try having a peer review after the first two days of development and again after the first week.
- **When can you demo it for me?** If the developer is resistant to other techniques, you can always try the old standby, "When can you demo it for me?" This causes the developer to provide you with and buy into their time estimate while recognizing that you will be evaluating some functional aspect of the project. So, if you are working on a new search filter, and the developer says he will be able to demo it by the end of the day Thursday, set up a meeting for

Friday at 9 a.m. right then and there to review the completed search filter with your developer.

So, with these techniques in mind, what would have been the right way to handle the vignette described in the beginning of this section?

- When outlining the task, the project manager should have specified that the developer spend no more than 2 hours on the project before checking in with him. If the company was using a task-tracking system, 2 hours should have been set as the initial maximum time.
- In addition, the project manager should have talked with the developer after the meeting, and been explicit about his expectations. If the developer thought that 2 hours was unrealistic, he would have had the opportunity to request more time for the project.
- If it was necessary to install and test each of the tools, the project manager could have created a line item in the budget for Existing Product Research and Evaluation. This way, the client would be able to appreciate the testing effort, and review the results with the project team to determine which, if any, of the three tools might be a good fit.

Handling Out-of-Scope Client Requests

No matter how well you gather requirements and identify the features of the project, new ideas will always come up during development. This is natural and impossible to avoid. The occurrence of these ideas does not mean that you failed to identify key requirements (though it can); rather, it is merely an organic part of the project development process.

It is unlikely that your client has ever gone through a thorough requirements gathering process before. Once they experience this process and begin to really spend time thinking about their project, other ideas will materialize. As the client talks about the project with colleagues and partners, other similar projects are likely to be mentioned, leading to still more ideas.

Your goal as the project manager is to ensure the project succeeds. The most common threat to a project is scope creep. If scope creep occurs, your project may fail. But, if you manage scope creep well, you can save your project's schedule, budget, and quality while keeping the client ultimately happy.

Here are the eight tricks to managing client requests like a hero.

Principle #1: Be Clear from the Start

It is vital to set the tone for how out-of-scope requests will be handled the first time the client makes such a request. Manage this correctly the first time, and every later request will be easy to handle.

Principle #2: Don't Stifle Enthusiasm

You do not want to stifle a client's enthusiasm when they have a new idea. So, respond positively and honestly. Be interested in the idea.

Principle #3: Don't Let Them Sit

There will likely be two kinds of requests. The first is for a modest change (1 to 4 hours) to an existing feature. The second will be far more complex and likely represent a new module, page or section. It is important to ensure that the feature request goes somewhere and does not sit unaddressed. For small changes, see Principle #4. For larger changes, see Principle #5.

Principle #4: Maintain a Feature Request List

When the first modest out-of-scope item comes in, take this opportunity to start the feature request list. This can be a simple spreadsheet that lists a short description of the request, who made the request, the date the request came in, and any reference to your internal issue tracking system (like a case number).

Your e-mail response should be clear that the feature request list is for out-of-scope requests that will be evaluated toward the end of the project if the budget allows. Once you start this list with one item, you can easily shepherd other out-of-scope requests to this document by simply writing, "I'll add this to the feature request list."

Principle #5: Do Not Be Afraid to Use Change Orders

Handle larger (more than 4 to 8 hours) out-of-scope requests with a change order. A change order is a simple document you use after a project has started to detail the cost of adding an out-of-scope feature to the project. When a feature request comes, respond with interest, but mention that it is a nontrivial modification, and ask if the client would like to see an estimate of the cost to implement this change.

A clear change order representing the cost of implementing an out-of-scope request allows the client to decide just how much they think this feature is worth. When it is free, the feature is always a good idea. When it has a price tag, things change.

For more information on change orders, see the next section, "Understanding Change Orders."

Principle #6: Resist the Urge to Do Everything

If you are the kind of person who likes to just take care of things (many call this type A), be aware that this will make it harder for you to manage scope creep.

Principle #7: It Will Not Be the Last Request

Our fearless project manager might find the urge to complete a modest refinement because he feels that this has to be the last request in the project. Do not do this, because it will not be the last. **The moment you feel like you just heard the last request is the moment the client decided to create ten more.**

Principle #8: Do Not Feel Bad

When the scope creeps in a project, you lose, the client loses, and the project loses. You might feel like you are being unhelpful by pushing away all requests, but a project free of creep tends to finish on time and on budget.

Understanding Change Orders

It is important to address four key points in a change order:

- The **Change Description** offers in plain English a concise description of the new features to be added to the project. A concise bullet-list would work as well.
- The **Schedule Impact** makes clear any changes to the project schedule.
- The **Design Impact** outlines any changes to the database or application architecture.
- The **Cost Impact** states the cost, usually in days of effort with your daily rate specified.

Most change orders can be short or, at most, two to three pages, and include these elements:

- A standard cover page you use for other documents, like scopes of work and requirements documents;
- The change description, and schedule, design, and cost impact section; and,
- The signature lines.

The change order serves several important purposes at this point:

- The change order documents exactly what tasks you and your client have agreed to, which will invariably be forgotten in a few weeks as the project progresses.
- The change order emphasizes that these changes really were out-of-scope.
- The change order emphasizes your team's contribution to the project, and clarifies any additional funds that your client needs to invest.
- Your client will likely be impressed that you are so methodical in your approach, especially if she has never seen a change order before.

Figure 5-1 details a real change order we prepared for NeonTommy.com, a Drupal development project to create an online news portal.

Change Description

A new set of features for the editorial control system were identified during a phone conference with the Annenberg Technology and Neon Tommy Editorial teams.

These new features relate to additional functionality with the site's main editorial control panel system, which is used to manage the story layout of the site home page and content section pages.

These new features include:

- Two new home page templates (for a total of five);
- The display of related stories on site and section home pages;
- Inclusion of the auto-populate tool at the box level during editorial actions;
- Refinement of the auto-populate tool logic to include the new story rank field;
- A gallery box for mixed multimedia content (any combination of videos, images and pod casts); and,
- A template box featuring "pod cast promos" to handle MP3 data.

Schedule Impact

This change request will not impact the project schedule.

Design Impact

This change order impacts the architecture for the system. The database schema and application architecture will be updated as needed to accommodate the new functionality discussed.

Cost Impact

The total cost for the implementation of this feature set is ▮▮▮▮ (▮▮▮▮ @ $1,000 per day).

Figure 5-1. A change order detailing refinements to NeonTommy.com

Negotiating Out-of-Scope Changes

If you do everything you can during the planning phase to manage the project team's expectations, document the project requirements, develop an appropriate budget, and allocate sufficient resources, the project should come in on time and on budget.

However, despite your best efforts, some aspects of the project can be interpreted differently by the client and consultant.

A Wretched Experience

We were building a custom web application that imported data on a nightly basis from the client's data management system, which we'll call WRETCHED. During the requirements gathering phase, we were told by the IT manager for WRETCHED that we would receive data in any format we specified. We priced the data import aspect of the project accordingly. However, during implementation of the project, the client's IT manager had moved on, and the new IT manager was only willing to export the data in the default system format. This change meant that instead of simply reading in the data file, we had to perform extensive preprocessing and data cleansing during the automated data import process. This effectively doubled the budget for this aspect of the project. From our perspective, this represented an out-of-scope change in the project. From the client's perspective, we had agreed to perform data import as part of the original project budget, and so it was in scope.

What did we do? We took a data sample from a similar project and a data sample from the client's WRETCHED data management system. To simplify the process for the client, we showed the client how one data set could be imported into Excel in a few steps. However, performing the same operation on the WRETCHED data set caused the import to fail. In the end, the client required her IT manager to provide data from WRETCHED in a standardized format or fund the additional work from the IT manager's budget.

Be Transparent

In our experience, the best approach is to be transparent and forthright about these issues when they emerge. Treating out-of-scope issues openly will ultimately build confidence with your client, as they realize that you are addressing matters head-on and not trying to just make them go away or cutting corners to get them done.

One of the recurring challenges with out-of-scope items is that the changes frequently come up throughout the course of a project. The temptation is to simply do the work, and move on. No one likes to disappoint a client by saying that something is out of scope. However, the better approach is to set aside tasks that you perceive to be out of scope, and tell the client that you will come back to that task at the end of the project. This way, you stay focused on completing the in-scope items on time and on budget.

As you near the end of the project, you will likely have a list (hopefully short) of out-of-scope items for discussion. However, by consolidating all of your out-of-scope items, you are in a stronger position to negotiate with your client.

Negotiating

Before you begin a conversation with your client, prepare a comprehensive list of all of the out-of-scope items that you have identified. Debating with your client about an 8-hour task on a $100K project might seem like you are nickel-and-diming your client. However, if you assemble a set of ten out-of-scope changes that represent 40 to 80 hours of additional work, this is a more sizable issue to discuss.

Addressing these issues with your client requires patience and finesse.

Tip The more calmly and professionally you approach negotiating unresolved out-of-scope changes, the more calmly and professionally your client is likely to respond.

You might explain to the client that it is in your team's best interest to maintain a positive relationship with them so that you can continue to benefit from working together in the long term. However, your development team also needs to remain profitable in order to continue to provide the services to all of your clients.

- First, try to figure out what seems equitable to you, and what fits in your budget. For example, if you have 80 hours of out-of-scope items on a project, and you propose to complete only 4 hours of the work, that is not likely to go over well with your client.

However, if you offer to complete 25% of the changes (20 hours), this might seem like a major concession to the client.

- You can either propose to take on those tasks that seem most important to you or you can let your client decide how to allocate those additional hours. If you let the client identify the top-priority tasks, you might be surprised to find that the items that you thought were most important to your client in the early part of the project actually turn out to be far less important by the end.
- You might also suggest that your client pay half the cost.
- Finally, you can suggest that any unresolved out-of-scope items can serve as the foundation for phase 2 of the project, which can begin as soon as phase 1 is done.

We find that this collaborative approach to negotiating out-of-scope changes works 90% of the time. The vast majority of clients understand that not all aspects of a project can be perfectly defined at the beginning—as anyone who has ever remodeled their kitchen or had their car repaired can attest.

What to Do in the Worst Case?

In the worst-case scenario, if your client simply refuses to negotiate and argues that all of the out-of-scope changes are, in fact, in scope, you have a difficult decision to make.

We find that conceding on the scope of work is a poor business decision. It leads your client to believe that they will always be able to push you to do extra work. Conceding the scope of work will also likely cause your project to be over budget. On the other hand, we take pride in leaving a project in the best possible state when we complete our work, and if there is still a lot of unbilled work, there may be considerable funds still on the table.

If you or your management team decide that you have to wind down the project at this point, we firmly believe that it is in your best interest to do this as gracefully and professionally as possible. First, meet with your team and explain the issue. Then, document the out-of-scope changes in a change order. Complete any remaining work, and let your client know that you have completed the current phase of the project and that you will need to wind down the project in an orderly manner at this point until the out-of-scope issues are negotiated. You can send along the change order and your project documentation. This act will signal to your client that you are acting professionally, despite the disagreement regarding the out-of-scope changes. This approach leaves the door open for future work or renegotiation.

Wrapping Up

Scheduling a project and managing out-of-scope client requests are vital to ensuring a successful project. You should now have a good sense of how manage these processes. In our next chapter, we look at how to overcome obstacles that often cause project delays.

We start off with the tale of an IT manager that fails to take ownership and subsequently loses control of resources. We then look at how to use a weekly checklist to maintain project momentum over the long weeks and months of a project. We wrap up the chapter by covering several techniques you can use to improve your interactions with and to facilitate the decision-making process of indecisive clients.

Running the Project

The Blindsided IT Manager

Todd is the IT manager for a department of 150 people within a Fortune 1,000 company. Like many IT managers, Todd feels that he and his five-member team are overworked, underappreciated, and underpaid, all of which might well be true. Todd is responsible for all IT purchases and projects in his department.

Three months ago, he was called into a meeting with one of the division directors (one of several bosses to whom Todd reports), and was asked to provide technical leadership on a new web-based application being worked on by another team of five staff members. The project had been approved by management to help track customers more efficiently. At the end of the meeting, Todd agreed to help define the project specifications and determine if the application should be hosted in-house or outsourced.

Of course, many more urgent projects had come up since then, and the customer-tracking system had been pushed down on his list. Although Todd had been quick to answer a few random questions from the project team via e-mail last month, he never found the time to schedule a follow-up meeting. In fact, the project sounded quite open-ended, so Todd was not entirely sure where to start. The lack of project definition made it easy for Todd to keep pushing this project down on his list.

Today, Todd was asked to attend a second project meeting. Expecting to be asked some technical questions, he reviewed the previous meeting agenda and his notes, and printed out the pricing for an online customer relationship management system he had heard positive things about at a recent technology conference.

During the meeting with the customer tracking team and the division manager, Todd feels blindsided as the team informs him that they have hired a consultant to develop the system and have already acquired the hardware. Todd will be responsible for getting the hardware set up in the division's data center and for supporting the hardware.

Todd is both embarrassed and angry. He had no warning that the team was moving forward without his advice. Further, the hardware that had been purchased was different from the type that Todd's division typically supported. Also, Todd noted defensively, the operating system and platform specified by the consultant would be totally new to the division, and he did not have anyone to support this system.

Todd is understandably upset, and he becomes increasingly defensive during the meeting. He knows from previous experience how to throw up techie-sounding roadblocks to a project, such as concerns about the scalability of a database technology. However, the team and the division director are patient and persistent. They offer to outsource the project hosting to the consultant and suggest that Todd can pay the hosting fees out of his IT budget.

By the time the meeting is over, Todd recognizes that he has lost control of this project. He had no idea that this project was so important and needed to move quickly, but he still finds it unconscionable that his director would move ahead without his advice. Todd decides that the best he can do now is provide the bare minimum support that has been requested of him while focusing his energies on more important and interesting projects.

Todd's biggest mistake was that he didn't take control of the situation after the initial project meeting. In the first meeting the leadership made it clear the project had funding and support and was moving ahead. At this point, Todd could have exerted more control over the destiny of his department by taking the lead on defining the project and hosting requirements.

His inaction left a vacuum of power that by necessity had to be filled by another person. It's unfortunate that others decided Todd's fate without consulting him, but by abdicating responsibility he is largely to blame. Indeed, had Todd spent a few moments after the initial meeting to think through what might happen, he may have guessed that losing control of his resources was a real risk and could have acted to stop that from happening.

In this chapter, we will introduce a series of techniques you can use to maintain project momentum, force answers from reluctant clients, and anticipate problems before they happen.

Maintaining Project Momentum

Momentum is critical in running a project. One reason projects slow down or stall is a lack of consistently applied attention to the project. It is easy to let a day go by when you do not move a project forward. The problem is that those days stack up because every additional day you do not give a project the attention that is needed, it gets easier to neglect. Before you know it, it has been weeks, work is piling up, and the real schedule for the project is behind.

The key to overcoming this challenge is **applying momentum**. We have two techniques for maintaining project momentum: one-a-day productivity and the Monday morning checklist.

Technique #1: One-a-day Productivity

The idea is simple: no matter how big the task or how many work hours it might take, simply complete one modest but measurable task each day that brings you one step closer to project completion. This task can be anything; just ensure that it is easy to quantify as a single unit of work. Maybe it is adding five testing checklist items to your quality assurance document, or quality assurance testing and verifying one new feature the developers completed. It does not matter, as long as it is one unit of work that brings you one step closer to completion.

When you start, it might seem like doing one modest unit of work will never have any impact on the massive task that is your project. But the old clichés—about how a journey is really just 10,000 steps, or how you can move a mountain by yourself if you are patient and move just one pebble each and every day—are true.

Take a recent personal project: Justin recently converted his modest DVD collection (about 250 discs). Digitizing a DVD does not take much effort—you put the DVD in the drive and click a few times on your computer—but you can only do one DVD at a time, and it takes your computer several hours to extract and transcode the movie to a computer-friendly video format. This was not a job he could knock out on a productive Saturday.

For several weeks, no DVDs got encoded. Why bother with one when there are so many to do? There is no hope!

Justin came up with a simple rule: encode one DVD a day. He was hesitant at first, as basic math shows this approach would take the better part of a year, but he persisted. Something funny happened right away. The easily attainable daily goal provided frequent motivation to "overachieve" and encode two or three DVDs per day. The DVDs got encoded in 3 months, and the daunting project went from overwhelming to complete.

When working on a project, a one-a-day approach fits in nicely with situations like working down a pile of bug fixes that need testing, verification, and review. A stack of 30 to 40 bug fixes is probably too much to do in a day, but if you set a goal of testing and verifying just two or three bugs a day, you can work down this list with speed. Or, set a goal to review one completed feature per day on a large project so that completed features from your developers do not overwhelm your Inbox.

The goal is simple: Doing several modest tasks consistently each day or week translates into a lot of progress over time.

Technique #2: The Monday Morning Checklist

The Monday morning checklist is likewise simple: it is merely a short list of tasks you complete each and every Monday morning. Why Monday? Monday is the best time to plan your and your team's priorities for the upcoming week. By identifying issues on Monday, you can allocate resources during the rest of the week to address those issues and solve any problems.

Monday is also the best time to look at the week's calendar and make sure that you are prepped and ready for upcoming meetings. (For all the same reasons, Monday is the best day to have individual team member meetings with your programmers, testers, designers, etc. Completing the checklist before these meetings is even better: you will have a good sense of where things stand and can set priorities for your team for the week.)

Justin first used the Monday morning checklist for a rather large project that lasted several months. The checklist itself was straightforward and included items such as the following:

- Are there any outstanding client action items that need follow-up?
- Are there any meetings this week that need prep?
- Review any completed features.
- Review and update the project schedule.

In all, there were about a dozen items that he could run through in under 1 hour. He ran through this checklist every Monday morning, and several benefits became clear:

- Meeting reminders went out and agendas were always ready for any upcoming meetings that week. There were no surprises, and the team was always prepared for meetings with the client.
- Any threats to the project schedule became apparent early.
- Feature review work did not pile up.
- Deliverables from the client were more consistently forthcoming (due to polite but persistent nagging).

The checklist forced him to prod the project forward each week and to keep chipping away in little pieces at the mountain of work it contained to keep the **project moving forward**.

It is likely you will have several smaller projects on your plate at any time, so you do not need a checklist for each one. In fact, the simpler your checklist, the better. Try putting together a single checklist that you run through each Monday that includes items for all of your ongoing projects.

Here are few tips for putting together a Monday morning checklist:

- Keep your checklist short. You need to complete this on Monday, a day when unexpected work tends to appear more frequently than the rest of the week. Include no more than 12 to 15 items.
- To reduce the chance you will gloss over a task, try to keep each checklist item specific and achievable. Do not include anything nebulous; only items with a clear path to completion belong on the checklist. You want to feel good after completing each one.
- Print it out, if possible. For whatever reason, crossing out items with a pen feels good. It is also harder to ignore a paper on your desk than a task item in Microsoft Outlook.

As an example, here is a Monday morning checklist Justin has been using recently (some specifics removed):

- Verify system administration checklist was completed last week. Review for any problems.
- Check on any past-due tickets.
- Review status of support tasks for {support project 1}, {support project 2}, {support project 3}.

- Schedule sanity checks. (In this context a *sanity check* is a checklist of things to review on a web application, such as server configuration, reviewing the log files, and targeting quality assurance tests.)
- Review billing report.
- Monthly: Send monthly summary to {client}.
- Review project schedule for {major project}.

Put Yourself in Your Client's Shoes

It's a powerful yet simple way to do good work: put yourself in your client's shoes. Most people do not do this—or think to do it—because our brains are not wired for it. But it is easy. When you are finished writing an e-mail but have not sent it, take your hands off the keyboard, take a deep breath and think, "OK, I'm the client. How does this read?"

You can also do this with the help of a colleague. I call it playing the devil's advocate.

Grab a colleague and say, "OK, I want you to be {client name}. Read this. What are your biggest concerns?" Guessing what people think is a fuzzy art. You will never be 100% accurate, but just the act of putting yourself in their shoes will work wonders for your perspective.

It is a great way to make sure you send decent e-mails. Try it for a week, and I promise that by Friday, you can look in your Sent box and notice the difference.

Proactive Project Management

From our experience, if clients are not responsive, their projects are behind schedule.

E-mails are an example. Responsive clients answer your e-mails quickly. They are probably the same clients that are easy to work with because they are comfortable making decisions.

By contrast, unresponsive clients do not make decisions, reply to your e-mails, answer your questions, or offer feedback. So, how can we persuade these clients to respond on their own initiative?

You cannot. There just is not a way to do this. That is where proactive project management comes in. Proactive management forces the client to decide. You tell the client you have evaluated an option and state very clearly that you will proceed with your option unless you hear back otherwise from him by a set deadline.

Here is a sample e-mail:

> Hi {client name},
>
> I'm happy to report that development of the new survey is going well. However, an issue has come up that I need your help with.
>
> We currently have the survey spread across 4 pages, as you outlined in your document. However, the questions on the third page of the survey are really short so the page looks out of place. I suggest we combine the questions from pages 2 and 3 and shorten the survey to just 3 pages (page 4 becomes 3).
>
> If I don't hear back from you by Friday I'll assume this works and we will proceed.
>
> Thanks,
> {call sign}

This approach is so very simple and so very effective because the client must decide whether to

- Not say anything, allowing you to proceed when you want and how you want;
- Give you a decision by your deadline so you can proceed; or,
- Say, "Hold on."

In our experience, option 3 happens rarely. Most of the time, the client will be silent, the project can proceed, and you can stay on time.

This is not a strategy to use on all clients, but it is helpful for many of them.

What Defensive Driving Teaches Us About Project Management

When Justin was a teenager and learning to drive, his mother offered him a single piece of very valuable advice: "Always assume everyone on the road is about to hit you. Look around at the cars and imagine ways that could happen. And then imagine what you would do to avoid it. That way, you can actively work to avoid it happening and be ready if it does."

This advice helps you drive more safely. When you think about the danger that other drivers pose, you start to develop safe driving habits; for example, looking in your mirror and deciding whether you have the clearance to suddenly stop or swerve to avoid something. In fast-moving cars, every second matters.

Project management may not be as fast-paced as driving, but the principle is the same. And this does not just apply to projects. It is the same advice that can help make everyone from butlers to chiefs of staff effective: try to plan for what is likely to occur and be ready for it before it happens. Whether being ready means making a cup of hot tea before being asked or having read a brief for a topic that *might* come up during a meeting, the result is the same: you are better able to handle a situation when you are prepared than when you are not.

In project management, being defensive means identifying what is likely to go wrong during and toward the end of the project. This is probably the original reason that all big project management tomes talk about creating massive risk assessment reports for documenting in detail all of the challenges a project might face (a veritable sea of pages and numbered outlines and indents and footnotes). But the problem with huge documents is just that: who has time to read a huge document?

You do not need to create a risk assessment document for your projects. However, you will benefit from taking a moment at the start of the project—and throughout—to think, "What is the biggest risk here, and what can I do right now to protect myself against it?"

- Try imagining **what each of the stakeholders is going to say when you show them the finished project**; not just your client sponsor, but the actual people who attend most of the meetings during the course of the project. These people are the driving force behind key features and sections. How do they think? Did they have a pet feature that did not fall within the scope?
- Try thinking about where in the project **the client might want changes**. This is probably going to be in one of the more complex features in the project.
- Try thinking back to previous **similar projects**, and recall what the main challenges were. Do any past lessons apply here?

- Were there any team members during requirements gathering and early scope discussions who proposed features that his or her internal organization ultimately decided against? This team member could feel **resentment**, which could poison their feedback and attitude in later phases of the project.

Hope for the best, prepare for the worst. Be defensive in your planning (but never in your composure to the client). Know that there will be some issue at the end of the project that you need to take care of, and make sure you have the capacity to do it. You have nothing to lose by planning ahead to handle an eventuality that has a real chance of coming to pass.

Planning ahead serves the interest of the client as much as it does the project manager and the firm for which you work; your project team will be ready to handle the situation, and the client's budget will be protected as well.

Quick Tips for Getting Work from Clients

Given that many clients tend to juggle lots of different projects simultaneously and with various different stakeholders (you are likely to be just one of many), it is sometimes hard to get the decisions and work product you need from your clients to move your project forward.

Here are some quick pointers to help mitigate this challenge:

- Use proactive project management (see "Proactive Project Management" earlier in this chapter).
- Do not be afraid to send a polite reminder to clients who have outstanding action item deliverables (see "Meeting Wrap-Up" in Chapter 3).
- Make deadlines and any delays to the schedule clear to the client in a polite way. When a deadline approaches, send a polite reminder that the project is going to be delayed if a deliverable or decision is not provided.

Be willing to accept a project delay from a client, but clearly state that the budget will be impacted to restart a project. Hopefully, your contract clearly states that restarting a project after a delay of a specific timeframe will incur project restart fees. If it does, you can gently mention that you really want to avoid having to put the project on hold and incurring those fees.

Wrapping Up

Maintaining project momentum is a major responsibility of any project manager. It's at the heart of what a project manager is meant to do: clear obstacles so others may get work done. Projects large and small need continual attention to move forward, step by step, toward a goal. Even if the step is small, the contribution to momentum is real. With what you've learned thus far, you now have a variety of techniques in your arsenal to address situations in your projects that can impact momentum.

In the next chapter, we look at an important step in the project planning process: the technical documentation. Where the requirements document outlines every feature that your project will contain, technical documentation details how each of those features will be implemented by your engineering team. While not every project needs technical documentation—and their length and density can often lead them to being underutilized—in preparing technical documentation you will encounter many of the technology challenges you would have encountered during development while still in planning.

As we have said many times already (and will continue to say), the earlier you are aware of the problem, the more cheaply (in hours or dollars) that problem can be addressed. Read on for guidance on when and how to write technical documentation.

Technical Documentation

By this time in the project, you should have a good set of requirements and a clear sense of the project features. You should also be able to confidently maintain project momentum and address common situations that cause delay. Now that you know what to build and how to keep the project moving, it's a good idea to first document the technical aspects of what your team is building.

Some technical documentation is meant to be shared with the client, and some is meant only for consumption by your project team. There are also many flavors of technical documentation—wireframes, design mock-ups, HTML mock-ups, and technical specifications, to name a few—so it's important to understand which documents are helpful when. What each format has in common is that they unify the concepts of what the project will be in a more visual and holistic manner than a dry bullet list of requirements could ever convey.

Technical documentation should not become a time sink. Ideally, it is another efficient step to help manage the expectations of the client and your team. In this chapter, we detail the most common types of technical documentation and guide you through how to create them.

In addition, we cover tips for how best to share work with your client, how to manage a design process that doesn't break the budget, and even how to create and document a database for a project.

Picking the Right Format

The first step in preparing technical documentation is identifying exactly what kind of documentation you need for your project. Let's start by looking at how you can pick the right format.

Design Mock-Up, Wireframes, and HTML Mock-Ups

A technical specification will assume different forms depending on the kind of project you are working on:

- In a **public web site project,** you are designing or redesigning the online presence of a company, organization, school, effort, project, or other group. In a public design project, the client will be anxious to see and provide feedback on the general look and feel and the branding of the site.
- In a **custom software project,** you are creating a web- or desktop-based application from scratch. In custom software, it will be critical to see how key screens will work, such as search tools, data input forms, and profile screens.

There are many different kinds of mock-ups you can prepare; these include the following:

- A traditional **design mock-up** is an image that shows how the project will look when finished, complete with the branding, colors, fonts, styles, visual flourishes, and sample content that will reflect the final project.
- A **wireframe** is a non-design structural mock-up that shows the visual order of elements on the page and how they relate to each other spatially. Wireframes do not include design elements like color, fonts, or images.
- A set of **HTML mock-ups** is a visual representation of how the site will look and flow. Links between the pages will work, form elements will generally be populated with typical values, colors and branding are present, and the main features of the site are shown.

In both a public website project and a custom software project, it is **best to prepare a set of wireframes and seek client approval before you prepare some kind of mock-up.** A visual mock-up (design or HTML mock-up) will take more time to create and more time to refine from client feedback than a wireframe, so it is helpful to nail down the core layout before the design phase.

A wireframe will also set the structure that the design mock-ups will need to follow, meaning the designer can focus on presenting the same structure visually in different ways. The client will be able to focus easily on the visual differences in the mock-ups, rather than the structural elements (which should already be set by the wireframes).

What is the **difference between a visual mock-up and a wireframe**? Take this example: a visual mock-up for a web site redesign project would include the logo being used for the project in the header of the mock-up. On a wireframe, the logo would likely be a square box labeled, "logo." See "Preparing Screen Mock-Ups" later in this chapter for some examples of wireframes and their resulting mock-ups.

Don't Mock Me Up

For a **public web site project** that does not involve much custom development, you can prepare a set of wireframes for client review. Once refined and approved, you can hand these wireframes and the requirements over to the designer, who can prepare the design mock-ups.

For a **custom software project,** there usually is not as much of a design component (beyond meeting the client's basic branding requirements) so much as an interactive design process. It is vital at this phase to show how the application will work, how the interaction between the user and the application will function, and how the screens will connect the workflow logically in the application. A set of HTML mock-ups will work best in this situation.

In a custom software project, the difference between individual pages will be much greater than the differences between individual pages in a public web site project, where the basic layout of content pages tends to be more consistent. Because of this, in a custom project you will need to create many more HTML mock-ups than traditional wireframes or design mock-ups.

For smaller custom software projects, a set of HTML mock-up screens (and the database schema, discussed later) are probably all you need for technical documentation. The developer will happily take the screens you prepared and start *building the business logic to support the implied functionality.* A good set of HTML mock-up screens for a smaller custom project can be so instructive that your developers might never open the requirements document during development.

The amount of detail you will need will vary. For **wireframes and design mock-ups**, prepare a home page and a sample content page. For **HTML mock-ups**, prepare a mock-up of every page, every form, every filter, and every control in the application.

Figure 7-1 details the HTML mock-up of a student database listing and search screen. Looking at the mock-up, you would not know that none of the functionality is present.

A clear set of mock-up screens has many benefits:

- The client probably will not understand fully what the project entails until seeing it rendered visually.
- Creating the mock-up screens makes preparing the database schema in tandem a snap (if applicable).
- The thought process that goes into the mock-ups will help expose any upcoming project challenges you have not yet anticipated, which will be easier to deal with before development has started.
- You can get the client to sign off on the visual representation of the application to help manage expectations.

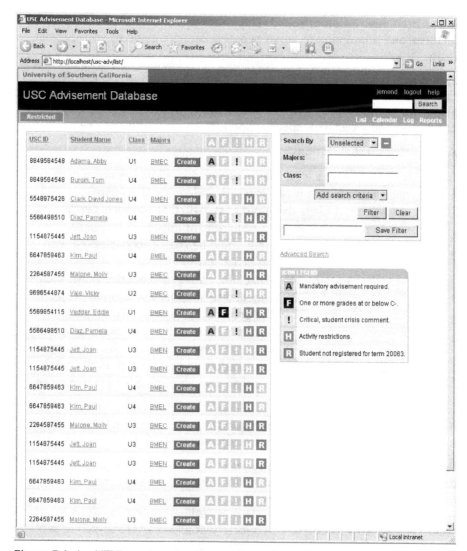

Figure 7-1. An HTML mock-up for the home page of a custom web application. The mock-up is just HTML; there is no functionality in the links and UI elements. (All data shown is random.)

When to Write a Technical Specification

For a more complex custom software project, you will need to prepare a **technical specification**. A technical specification is actually quite simple. It is a written description of your HTML mock-ups and of all of your project's features, and is intended to serve as a development guide to your project team.

A technical specification describes everything that goes on *behind the scenes* or that is not immediately apparent in your HTML mock-ups. A spec is most helpful for complex or larger custom software projects. A good way to find out if you need a technical specification is to look at your requirements.

Ask yourself these questions:

- Is there business logic that is required as a foundation to certain requirements that is not explicitly called out as its own requirement? Or is there business logic that supports certain requirements, but is not a requirement itself?
- Are there requirements that could be reasonably achieved with vastly different technical approaches?
- Are there requirements that affect other project decisions, such as the server configuration needed to support the finished project?
- Is there functionality in the project that is unfamiliar to your development team or unlike previous work your team has done?
- Is this project generally larger and more complex than projects completed successfully, on schedule and on budget, in the past?
- Will the project take more than a week of time, or involve more than one programmer?[1]

If you answered yes to any of these questions, then you probably need a technical specification. Let's look at an example.

Say you have a project to build a series of web forms for editing structured data such as contact records. The HTML mock-up screens you prepare will make it clear where fields go, how the forms are laid out, and how the workflow will work. Additionally, there is really only one way (in a specific technical platform) to create a web form that allows users to edit data. There is not much in the way of discussion or possibilities of "gotchas" in building this kind of project.

However, if you also have a series of requirements to build an e-mail new-sletter system into the contact database then you need a technical specification. Why? Because there will be many **technical decisions that your**

---

[1] Joel Spolsky, "Painless Functional Specifications," www.joelonsoftware.com/articles/fog0000000036.html, October 2, 2000.

programmers will have to make in order to build an e-mail newsletter system that would not be addressed in the requirements document.

Here are just a few questions: How will e-mails be sent? Will they be queued and sent by an automated process, or sent immediately? Will the process run hourly, daily, every 10 minutes? How will we handle the processes running over each other? How will the process be set up on the server? Do we need a separate machine for handling the queue? How will we handle bounces? Prunes? Unsubscribe requests? Do we need to make any DNS changes so our e-mails do not get flagged as spam?

Too many unanswered questions are deadly to a project. Leaving the wrong kind of decisions to your programmers (and not answering them up front) will likely cause problems of budget, scope creep, schedule, scalability, and fault tolerance (often a challenge in e-mail systems) in your project.

Figure 7-2 is a real technical specification for a large, internal, custom ASP.NET project for a major university.

6.3 Student Advising Subsystem

Figure 32: Student advising screenshot

6.3.1 Student Advisement Program Tabs

At the heart of the application is the student advising subsystem, which organizes all advisement activity by the major, minor or special program (all three of these categories are hereafter referred to as just program) of the student being advised.

For each student program record there is a corresponding tab after the four primary student navigation tabs that link to the student advisement history pages for that program. The name of the tab is the short code (three to four characters) name for that program.

Each program's history page is identical in form and function and different only in content.

6.3.2 Student Advisement History Page

About the Section

The student advisement history page is a collection of all advisement activity for a particular student-program combination. Advisement activity includes:

- Academic review forms
- Advisement sheets

Figure 7-2. A page from a technical specification detailing how a key user interface element will work

All Together Now

To bring it all together, here is what to use when and where and how:

- A **design mock-up** is an image that shows exactly how a typical page will look. Best used for public web design projects.
- A **wireframe** is a non-styled mock-up of how the major elements of a web page will be arranged and positioned in relation to each other. Good for most projects before design mock-ups or HTML mock-ups are created.
- An **HTML mock-up** is a clickable set of screens that work in a browser and look exactly how the application will look. Best used for custom software development.
- A **technical specification** is a plain-language document that describes in detail what every part of every page will do and typically contains screen shots of the HTML mock-ups. Best for larger custom software projects.

For a typical public design web project, the process would be

1. Collect requirements

2. Prepare wireframes

3. Collect feedback and refine

4. Prepare design mock-ups

For a typical midsize custom software project, the process would be

1. Collect requirements

2. Prepare wireframes

3. Collect feedback and refine

4. Prepare HTML mock-ups

For a typical larger custom software project, the process would be

1. Collect requirements

2. Prepare wireframes (optional)

3. Collect feedback and refine

4. Prepare HTML mock-ups

5. Collect feedback and refine

6. Prepare technical specification

7. Prepare database schema (see "Creating a Database" later in this chapter)

Preparing Screen Mock-Ups

This guide is not about the design process, so we will not delve into tips on the art of design (which is a good thing, because we do not have any). However, here are some general pointers that will help make the mock-up phase a breeze.

For custom software projects:

- **Focus on the workflow**. When conceptualizing what screens need to be in the application, try to think in terms of what needs to get done, rather than thinking about what screens might need to exist. Let the workflow of the user guide you.

- Show any key screens, such as search forms and input forms, complete with all of the fields you expect to include. This will make the workflow very clear to the client and will help catch any misconceptions.

- Imagine yourself in the office of your client trying to get some work done. How is this tool going to fit into your workflow and make it faster?

- Find a great design to inspire you. There is nothing wrong with starting the mock-up process by finding an application interface that you feel does a great job solving a problem similar to the one your project hopes to solve. Start by building up your first screen by copying the design, and then let it evolve.

- In each project where you design custom interfaces, **try to make one specific, measurable improvement** in this mock-up over your previous projects. This might be taking an element you often include and making it better by trying something new. This might mean changing the paradigm under which you define the navigation of the application. Whatever it means is not important, as long as you are trying with each project to do something new, which, in the process, becomes something better.

- Run some **informal usability tests** (sometimes called "hallway usability tests"). Grab a nontechnical member of your organization and put them in front of the mock-up. Point to an area on the mock-up and say, "What will this do if you click here?" Or ask questions about how to do a certain workflow, like, "Where do you go to search by last name?" The answers will be revealing.

For **public web site design projects,** it is most helpful to have a great checklist of questions to ask in the requirements gathering phase about design, such as

- What are some examples of web sites with designs you like?
- What are some examples of web sites you don't like?
- What colors should we use and not use?
- Do you have existing logos and designs we can use as a basis for the design?
- Do you have any branding or identity requirements?
- Do you want the navigation to appear horizontally across the top or vertically down the left side?
- Do you want a fixed or fluid layout?

When the wireframes are ready, send them to the client to review and set up a meeting to discuss them. Begin the meeting by explaining what each element in the wireframe represents. This helps ensure that everything is clear to the client.

Let's look at several examples. The wireframe in Figure 7-3 was for a dashboard for nonpublic users on a news-driven site. This is really a web application design exercise and not a public web site design exercise, and this page was part of a larger suite of tools to facilitate running a news site. This wireframe was created using Balsamiq Mockups, a wireframing software tool. Figure 7-4 shows the real web page that resulted from this initial wireframe.

USC ASC NeonTommy.com Drupal Development

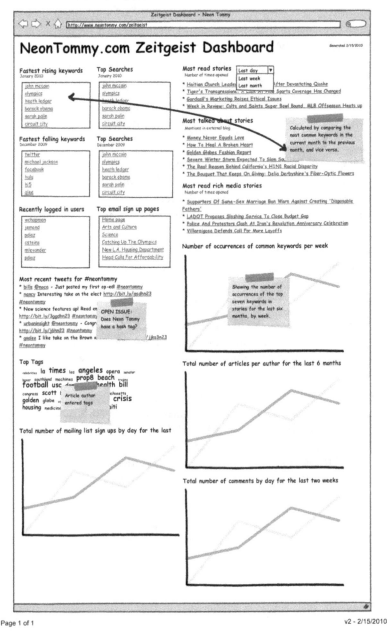

Figure 7-3. A wireframe for the editor's site activity dashboard in NeonTommy.com

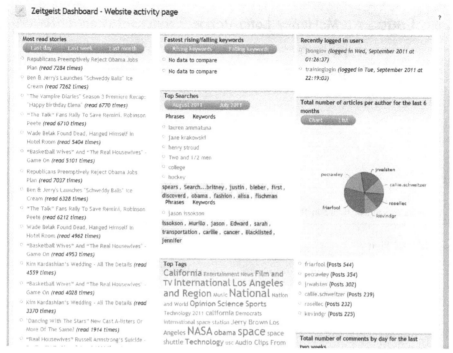

Figure 7-4. The wireframe in Figure 7-3 was turned into this real web page, called the Zeitgeist Dashboard.

The wireframe in Figure 7-5 was for a web development project whose goal was to encourage public participation in the McHenry County, Illinois, 2040 Long Range Transportation Plan. This wireframe was created by Urban Insight project manager Chris Loos using Mockups. Figure 7-6 shows the homepage.

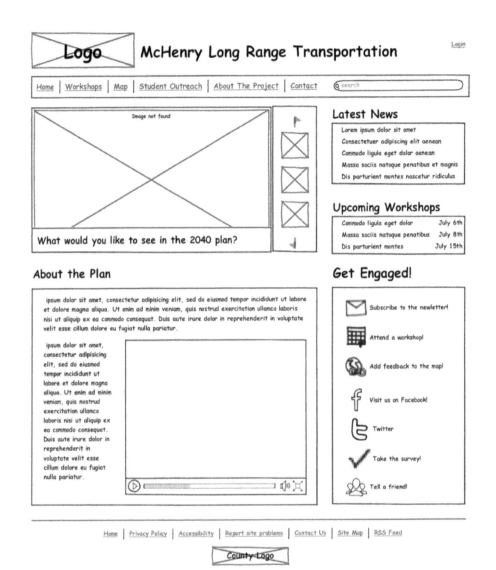

Figure 7-5. A sample homepage wireframe for a web site to encourage public participation

Figure 7-6. A sample design for the McHenry County, Illinois, 2040 Long Range Transportation Plan created based on the wireframe

The wireframe in Figure 7-7 was created to specify a web-based video gallery for the Los Angeles County Museum of Art. This wireframe was created by Urban Insight project manager Kurt Rademakers, PMP, using Microsoft Visio, which is often favored by project managers who have to create many wireframes that share common elements. The web page is shown in Figure 7-8.

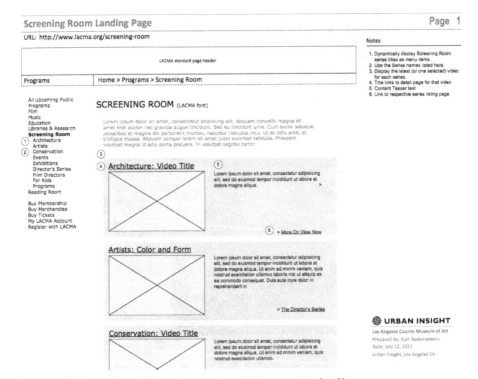

Figure 7-7. A sample wireframe for a web site to present a video library

Figure 7-8. The implemented video library page based on the wireframe

In this case, because a clearly defined design for the web site already existed, the project team went directly from wireframes to implementation.

Sharing Your Work with the Client

It is important to present the wireframes and mock-ups to the client in a **professional manner**:

- Mock-ups are typically exported by a designer in an image format. Consider posting a simple but clean page on your web site (with a private URL) to post them.
- As they are produced, you can post newer versions of the mock-ups at the top of your private page, pushing the older comps down the page chronologically. This provides an easy way to see the progress of refinements and make it clear which is the most current design.
- Show a large thumbnail of each comp that links to a nice, crisp, full-size image.
- Label each mock-up to provide names that can be used by your clients when discussing specific mock-ups.

When preparing wireframes to share with the client, consider the following:

- Export the wireframe as a PDF, not a PNG. PDFs open and display reliably in Adobe Reader, which is widely available on most platforms. PNGs do not reliably open in an application that offers easy review.
- Clean up any extra attributes your wireframe software adds to the PDF. Anything that is not directly related to the wireframe and that might confuse your client should be removed.
- Change the properties of the PDF so that the document opens to show the entire first page.
- Add a header to the PDF with the project title, wireframe title, date, and version number.
- For multiple-page wireframes, add the page number in the footer.

NOTE   See the Appendix for neat wireframe and mock-up tools that we have found helpful.

The Design Process

The visual design aspect of a web site development project tends to be the most fun for both you and your client, but it also has the potential to throw the project off track. Let's face it: design is subjective. We have seen perfectly professional and usable designs destroyed by a committee of non-design professionals who all wanted to add their own signature touches during the design review process.

Here are several subtle tactics for keeping the visual design aspect of your project on track.

- Try to remove some of the subjectivity in design by creating two sample home page wireframes before you create the design, so clients can focus on the placement of elements first.
- Include a "design brief" in your requirements gathering process. Recall that a design brief captures the key design requirements about the project, and determines the known design constraints such as the use of logos, whether the page width is fluid or fixed, and other design requirements.
- Review a series of ten preselected designs (not necessarily yours) of well-designed sites, and spend time discussing them. In the process, the client learns something about site design and you learn what they like.
- If you are working with a committee, perform this design discussion with the committee and ask them to reach consensus on the elements they do and do not like. The committee will perceive design development as a collaborative process. Otherwise, if you develop the design without their participation, you increase the risk they will reject it when you present it.

Because it is subjective, the design process can go on for a long time unless you constrain it. The best way to do this is to be explicit about what the design process will include and associate a cost with continued design revisions. Here is a model that we have found can work well:

- Agree to prepare three different initial design mock-ups. These will be based on the client's design goals, wireframes, and a review of other well-designed web sites.
- In addition to the initial design, conduct two rounds of design review and modification based on client feedback.
- State that each round of design review can be replaced by another new or fresh design if the client does not like one of the original three.
- After the home page design is set, create one or two content page designs, which typically reflect the design of the home page.

- Perform one round of design review and modification of the content page designs.
- State that further design refinements will be subject to a time-and-materials fee. Obviously, you can decide to be more lenient and waive the fee for additional designs or rounds of design, but at least you have clearly defined the expected process.

After you have created the initial set of three designs, it is often useful to schedule at least one and probably two design review meetings with your client to carefully walk through each of the designs. Most designers create the initial designs as images using Photoshop or Illustrator, with the mock-ups presented as images on a web page, emulating the look of the finished web site. This presentation can confuse clients, leading them to believe that the application or web site is already completed.

During your design meeting, it is useful to cover the following points:

- Remind the client of the process you used to get here. For example, "These designs are based on the wireframes, design brief requirements, and the review of ten selected designs."
- Explain that the designs are images, not actual web pages.
- Walk through the header and navigation placement in each design.
- Identify and discuss how each interactive feature is envisioned to work on the finished application. Many web-savvy project managers gloss over elements of the design that seem obvious to them, but which the client may not understand. For example, a series of social media icons may imply to you that these icons link to social media sites, but unless you state this explicitly, the client may not understand why the icons appear on the design.

Here are a few additional things we have learned over the years:

- Don't be defensive. Or, if you have your visual designer or team participating in the meeting, be sure to alert them not be defensive. Clearly explain each and every aspect of the design, but if the client is negative about some aspect of a design, simply note that. Try hard not to argue with the client about the designs. This puts you in a defensive position, instead of being the client's advocate through the design process.
- Unless you happen to be a design expert (many project managers are not), try to withhold your subjective opinions about the designs

unless explicitly asked. Instead, try to point out differences among the designs that the client should notice.

- As you proceed through the design meeting, collect the feedback in a written form, so you can present the feedback to your visual designer or team.

- As you wrap up your design meeting, be certain to summarize the feedback you have collected, and briefly explain the next step in the design process. This will help to build confidence with your client that you have understood the feedback, but that the design review is still proceeding inside the overall design process that you already have defined.

Be patient, positive, clear, and concise, and with a little luck, your design process will move ahead flawlessly.

Creating a Database

Creating the database for your custom project should be a very satisfying phase for three important reasons:

- It feels like an accomplishment;
- It looks impressive when printed; and,
- It gives you a strong sense of how the entire application will work at a technical level.

Some technical project managers may be up to the task of creating a database schema for the project on their own. However, database design is not likely to be part of the skill set of most project managers.

If you have limited or no experience with database design, you may want to work alongside a developer to create the database schema or delegate this task to an experienced developer, and have her walk you through the schema she creates.

We do find that project managers should be involved in the database design phase, as it provides three unique benefits:

- It makes the project manager acutely aware of how requirements relate to database design.
- He gets a much deeper understanding of the application you are building.

- He can offer greater insight about how the requirements relate to the data structure.

In most cases, it is easiest to build the database schema after you complete and refine the HTML mock-ups. The mock-ups will go through several revisions, following internal and external feedback, so starting the schema too early may waste time with needed revisions. Once the mock-ups are completed, you can design the database alone or in tandem with writing the technical specification (if you are writing one).

For a project that will not have a technical specification, you can simply go through the HTML mock-ups one at a time and create the necessary database structure for each page in the application. If you are writing a technical specification for the project, write the database schema at the same time. This will help you conceptualize the *technical architecture* of the application.

As when designing the schema for a project with just mock-ups, try building the parts of the database needed to support each section as you write the technical specification.

Here are some general tips that can help with the database phase, whether you are doing it yourself or working with a developer:

- **Create the database schema in the same database** being used for the project. Written schemas on paper do not evoke the same thought process as creating it in reality. Besides, in most database management systems, it is less time consuming to do it this way.
- Think in terms of how the database will support a feature during requirements gathering. This will speed up the process of database design and help shape the technical architecture of the project in your head.
- Think or talk through a feature completely, start to finish, and identify every piece of schema needed.
- Seek out problems in how the schema will support a feature. You will likely find problems that can be solved much more cheaply now than later in the development process.
- Identify whether your application is more read-heavy or write-heavy, and structure your data accordingly.

Why bother creating the database schema before you start development? As with writing a technical specification, creating the actual database needed to support all features in the site will likely reveal technical issues you need to discuss with your team and solve now, before development starts. Fixing a problem during development takes more programming hours and costs more money than if it had been fixed earlier. The most expensive line item in your project budget is likely human hours; guard them jealously.

Writing a Specification

A technical specification describes everything that goes on *behind the scenes* or is not immediately apparent in your HTML mock-ups. The spec should include screenshots of the prototype screens you prepared. This is important when you have a more complex interface with lots of business logic.

This is also a good place to set the tone for the technical architecture and basis from which your developers will write code. Before any coding starts, you can protect the project development from going down paths that are likely to lead to scope creep, poor performance, or scalability issues.

The technical specification document is a companion document to your database schema and your HTML mock-ups, and it typically should include both the schema and mock-ups. It should restate any features mentioned in the requirements document and any functionality implied in the HTML mock-ups, such that the entire set of project requirements exists in the technical specification. Why? Because your developers—no matter how hard you try—will only begrudgingly read one document. You want it to be the technical specification.

The Meat and Potatoes

A basic technical specification includes the following elements:

- Functional description for each module (the meat and potatoes)
- The database schema
- Lots of screen shots of your HTML mock-ups

The pieces of a basic specification are straightforward and include the biggest section by far: the functional description. The functional description should be littered with screen shots from your HTML mock-ups and references to the database schema.

Essentially, this section should step through each major part of the application and describe, in plain language, every little thing the application will do.

Just pick the first page of the application, paste in a screen shot, and start describing everything on this page.

- Describe everything that is left unsaid, even the components you *assume* are implied by the mock-ups, but are not clearly visible. The less ambiguity, the better.
- Use the principles of good web writing in your spec: clarity and brevity, **lots of bullet points**, and **selective bolding**.
- Mention the specific database tables and fields that will supply data to various parts of the application.
- Carefully **explain the logic that manages the state of a multi-state object**, such as context-based buttons, rich data display tables, and drop-down menus.
- Look for **logic patterns** in the application that will lend easily to creating centralized logic for common routines. The principle of DRY—*Don't Repeat Yourself*—is often a valuable timesaver.

The full database schema can appear at the end of the specification, in an appendix. For example, Microsoft SQL Server Management Studio includes a handy tool to visually define the primary-foreign key relationships between tables. Screenshots of these diagrams clearly convey how the schema supports the project's functionality.

Think Through a Feature

Consider the entire life cycle of a feature by thinking through all of its implications. This helps you identify any potential "gotchas" that will impact the schedule, scope, and challenge of a task.

Some questions you might ask:

- Does this feature impact search?
- Will the data captured by this feature accumulate over time and need to be trimmed?
- How is this feature used in other (secondary) areas of the application? Will the current method of implementation cause a reduction in performance?
- What might this screen look like after 6 months of data? A year? Three?
- How could this feature be used incorrectly?

- Does this involve a fixed list of values? If so, where are they defined, how are they stored, and how might these values change over time?

Be Specific: An Example

The single most important task in writing a technical specification is to ensure specificity.

The following is an extract from a technical specification for a web site project that involved a complex custom events registration system. This section describes an information box at the top of the user profile page, referencing the specific fields in the database where this information resides:

The user homepage for registered members includes a small information block at the top of the page and an events listing below. The information block displays

- General eligibility status
- CAP eligibility status
- CAP certification status

    - Indicates whether a user has attended a CAP orientation event
    - Checks whether person actually attended event

- Last CAP workshop date (from Attendee and Event table)
- Next available CAP workshop date
- Number of events missed in last 12 months
- A link on the homepage takes the member to a page to view and update all information from the member registration form (see above)

This next example is from the same project and describes the logic that defines what appears in an RSVP column of a table of upcoming events presented to a logged-in user:

The Status/RSVP column:

- Shows an RSVP button for events that member is eligible for and that are not full
- Shows an "Add to wait list" button when the user is eligible and an event is full
- Shows "RSVP'ed" if the member is RSVP'ed for the event

- A Cancel button appears next to RSVP'ed if the current time is before midnight of the night before the event
- When a user presses Cancel, the next available wait list attendee (based on the date and time added to the wait list) is changed to attendee and sent an e-mail alert:

Congratulations! Due to a cancellation, you have been moved from the wait list to an attendee for [EVENT NAME] on [EVENT DATE AND TIME].

Login at http://example.org for complete event details.

- Changes to CAP eligibility (see outlined Event Eligibility section)
    - If an attendee is being added to a CAP workshop-type event, then a CAP ineligibility date is added to the member record for 90 days after the date of the event.
    - If the attendee is being added to a CAP orientation-type event, a CAP eligibility date is set to the date of the event.
- When the event is within 24 hours, system outputs, "Please call to cancel your reservation."

- Shows "Wait list" if the member is on the wait list
- Shows "Ineligible" if the user is not eligible for the event, and the reason why
- Shows "Call to book" if a user is eligible for the event, the event is not full, the user is not RSVP'ed or on the wait list, and the event date is within 24 hours

The Status/RSVP button uses eligibility logic outlined in the Event Eligibility section to control for which events the member may register.

The detail in these examples may look excessive, but these questions need to be asked and answered before the project starts, as part of the requirements document (See "About Requirements" in Chapter 4). If they are not, then programmer hours will be spent fixing these issues after primary development is complete, when it is much more time-consuming to make changes.

The Side Dishes

The additional sections of your technical specification will likely be defined by the requirements of the project and might include sections like the following:

- Data imports (if relevant)2
- Application architecture
- Server/hardware infrastructure
- Development/coding standards (sometimes useful if new employees are on the project team)
- Security considerations

For a larger custom development project, it is helpful to talk a little about the application architecture:

- How will you approach organizing the various elements of whatever language you choose, like functions, methods, classes, and objects?
- Where will the business logic reside?
- Will you use an existing application framework?
- How will you set up a testing environment to support development of tricky features like e-mail or billing systems?

The servers supporting the project will also impact development and should be stated clearly:

- How many servers?
- What will be the software and hardware stack of each server?
- Will they all be behind the same firewall in the same network, or will they be separate?
- Will they be physically separated, with the Internet in between?

If your team has new members, clearly (and briefly) explain how your shop develops software. An experienced team will have made the mistakes that less-experienced programmers tend to make, and will avoid them. But you cannot assume that new members will have had the same experiences.

Finally, consider if there are any security implications in your application:

---

[2] Data imports are almost always harder than you expect. Protect your project budget by throwing a lot of detail and planning into the data import before development starts on any part of the application.

- Are there privacy laws (like HIPAA or FERPA in the United States) that impact your application?
- Do you have data in your database that should never make it into log files or debugging routines?
- Do you need to encrypt the login credentials stored in your code?
- Do you need to encrypt the database?

More Reading

See the Appendix for some great additional reading on writing a technical specification. If you have time to read only one additional article, read Joel Spolsky's "Painless Functional Specifications."

Wrapping Up

Your planning is done. By now you should have a strong sense of all of the documentation you need for your project, be it requirements documents, HTML mock-ups, wireframes, designs, technical specifications, or database schemas. It's now time—at long last!—to cash in all of your hard work and begin development.

In the next chapter, we cover everything you need to know to keep your sanity during the development phase. We start with a horror story about a developer going rogue. We cover guidance on how to keep your client in the loop, tips for writing professional e-mails, and easy ways to maintain documentation.

We go over the simple but powerful method of using checklists to maintain quality and show you how to avoid the crippling nature of no-win-scenario bugs. We wrap up the chapter by detailing how to conduct weekly developer meetings that keep your team happy and your project on track.

Development, Communication, Documentation

A Developer Out of Control

Jack is a web developer for a ten-person consulting firm. Although he has no formal training in computer science, he has 5 years of development experience with a range of open source tools and is passionate about his work. Jack is tasked with building a new web application to accept advertisements for an online publication. Because the client's contact is familiar with web development technologies, Jack tells his project manager he is willing to serve as the client liaison and work directly with the client on a daily basis. As usual, he will check in with his project manager each week to provide a status update.

The project starts out very well. Jack is on budget, and the client is happy. The consulting firm's project manager begins to give Jack more leeway because everything is moving along so smoothly, and decides to have meetings every other week.

Jack really likes the application he is developing and decides to try a new development framework. Because this is really a technical decision, he does not feel that he needs to get clearance. Jack is off and running. About a month into the project, he notices a couple of features that could really improve the user experience and suggests them to the client. The client is excited about the improvements and makes a few recommendations of his own. Jack means to make a note of these changes and tell his project manager about them, but on the day of their regular progress meeting—which now takes place every 2 weeks—the project manager was away at a training session. However, the changes are not that big, so he decides he can remember them all.

Jack keeps plugging away. Some minor technical glitches crop up between the framework he decided to use and a few of the improvements he and the client agreed to implement. However, he finds a workaround with only a couple of days' worth of extra effort.

One afternoon, the client calls Jack and excitedly tells him that the prototype system is so popular that two new clients have signed onto the project, so they will need to extend the application to enable clients from multiple magazines to use the system. Initially, Jack is nervous about this new technical direction because some of the previous modifications, combined with this new requirement and his selection of a new framework, are causing some technical problems.

Jack lets deadlines on other projects slip by as he tackles one problem after another. He always feels like he is just a day or two from being done until a new problem or bug creeps in.

Jack's project manager hastily calls a meeting to discuss the missed deadlines on several other projects; it has now been nearly 4 weeks since their last meeting. Jack proudly demonstrates all of the new features and increased functionality he has built into the system—including a few graphical flourishes of his own—and explains that he is very close to solving his latest technical issue. Finally, he discloses that the new coding framework he selected is causing a few problems.

He notices that his project manager is becoming increasingly agitated. The project manager explains that Jack is already 20% over budget on the project and cannot understand why he has adopted a new development framework on his own—one that no one else at the consulting firm uses—which means that Jack is effectively the only person who can continue working on this project. To Jack's surprise, the project manager tells him to stop work on the project while he calls a meeting with the company's management to determine how to proceed.

In this case Jack and the project manager are both at fault. Jack overstepped his role as a developer, and the project manager allowed this to happen. It is exceptionally hard for a developer who is deeply involved in the details of programming a system to clearly understand the broad context into which his work will fit. This is an important role for the project manager. When the project manager and developer don't clearly and consistently communicate, problems can emerge rapidly.

This chapter offers guidance on keeping the project team on track and ensuring that documentation is being prepared as the team progresses.

Keeping the Client Updated

It is likely that the bulk of the project schedule will be taken up by the development phase, which involves little communication between you and the client. This is normal if it happens, but it is essential to provide regular updates to the client during this period.

A simple e-mail, sent once a week, is sufficient to keep the client updated on the status of the project. Keep the e-mail brief and mention a few specific milestones that have been completed, the major upcoming milestones, and reconfirm the launch date of the project (if it is still on track).

It is also likely that during the development phase you will hit upon an issue that requires some client input to resolve. This is an opportune time to bring the client into the decision process. To protect against the unexpected or the unwise suggestion, be sure to frame possible solutions as specific options in an e-mail, and request a decision on the option the client feels is best. You might consider scheduling a brief conference call to discuss the issue at hand, beginning the call with a quick project status update.

Bringing the client into a guided decision has several benefits:

- The client feels like part of the project process.
- The client gets to buy into the decision. This helps to manage expectations about the issue at a later date, as they were part of the decision-making process.
- The project is protected by defining the possible solutions from the start. This helps ensure that no options do more harm than good overall.

Replying Quickly

An easy way to keep a client satisfied and confident in the project process is to reply to e-mails in a timely manner. If the client sends a note about a problem, reply quickly that your team is investigating the issue and identify when you will update them next. A quick reply will be appreciated and alleviates any pressure on the sender (say, if she is receiving pressure about the issue from her own internal team).

Because people usually are slow to respond to e-mails, your client will appreciate a prompt reply. It is an easy, low-cost way to make a positive impact on your client.

For more details, see "Be Responsive" in Chapter 11.

Tips for Writing E-mails

Love it or hate it, e-mail has become the dominant mode of communication among teams in business. Like any tool, an e-mail can be used well or poorly. Let's look at how to use e-mail effectively.

Professionalism

Because e-mails have such low cost (easy to write, free to deliver, instant arrival), the written quality of e-mail tends to degrade to simple, curt messages. Resist this temptation. An e-mail to a client should be complete, spelled correctly, short, and relevant.

Here are our e-mail tips:

- Start the e-mail with a friendly "Hi {Name}" or "Hi Team" when addressed to several people.
- Be polite; for example, use "kindly" and "thanks for your note."
- Limit the e-mail to three or four paragraphs.
- Limit paragraphs to three or four sentences.
- Take time to write a simple, respectful and professional e-mail— even in response to one-line e-mails. In doing so, you maintain a professional demeanor and make clients appreciative.

What's in a CC?

A CC on an e-mail is one of two things:

- A way to keep a team member informed; or,
- A handy way to lend weight to an e-mail by keeping the boss informed.

While a BCC is a soft notification (in that you let the boss know something without the recipient's knowledge), a CC is a hard notification in that it adds authoritative weight to any e-mail sent. A BCC is used to let a valued employee save face while still keeping the boss in the loop. A CC is used to reinforce the e-mail with the superior authority of the person CC'ed.

When used correctly, a CC can say, "Hey! This is important, as I am letting the boss know I told you this."

Don't Be Rude

Do not be rude in e-mails. Do not place blame, and do not write something to make your wounded self feel better. Try to be unflappable.

If you are writing to check in on a client who has not responded or who has dropped the ball on something, say something like, "I just wanted to check in on the {whatever project}. If there is anything I can do to help, kindly let me know."

Your Vacation Auto-Response Message Is Probably Wrong

Most people do not set up e-mail vacation auto-replies correctly and typically commit a few usability gaffes in these auto-responders.

Here are few helpful guidelines when configuring your auto-response:

1. Be absolutely clear to the reader exactly what date you are back at your desk reading e-mail.
2. Recipients should only receive a repeat response once every 5 days.
3. Include coverage contact information: who can the reader contact while you are away if they need help?
4. Always include the original subject line in the auto-response e-mail.

5. Avoid stating when you started your vacation; focus on when you will return and be available.

Guidelines 1 through 3 are a simple matter of **professional manners and responsibility**.

Guideline 4 is important for two reasons: including the original subject line reminds the recipient of the source e-mail that generated the message (and thus roughly what date they discovered you were on vacation). In addition, including the subject line decreases spam when vacation responses are sent to e-mail addresses that feed into issue-tracking systems.

Guideline 5 keeps the client focused on when they might expect a reply, rather than thinking about your wonderful vacation.

The Power of Checklists

A checklist is a simple little thing: a list of items written in a meaningful order. Beyond your own lists for the grocery store and for preparing for travel, you are surrounded by a variety of invisible checklists that keep you safe, secure, and happy.

For example, say you are taking a two-hour flight from Boston to Washington, DC. This trip seems routine from the passenger's perspective, with a short flight, nice flight attendants (maybe), and an easy landing. But this is made possible by trained professionals piloting a marvel of engineering that took decades to design, billions of dollars to build, and requires thousands of small mechanical components to work in concert. The complexity of a commercial airliner is made abundantly clear to us lay people if we catch of glimpse of the cockpit control deck, complete with hundreds of dials, knobs, switches, readouts, and gauges. And yet at the end of a flight, you are still alive and the pilots do not seem all that stressed while standing in the cockpit door and saying goodbye to deplaning passengers.

How is all of this possible? A myriad of factors, really: government regulations, the wide use of safety technologies, modern computers, and increasingly sophisticated airplanes. And, of course, one more important piece of safety is the preflight checklist. If you ever saw the pilot looking at a clipboard before the plane departed, she was probably running through the preflight checklist.

This checklist includes steps to verify everything from having enough fuel to the right oil levels to testing critical components. These checks might seem obvious, but there are dozens of them, and one or two can be easily overlooked. Most often, the checklist does not find any problems, but pilots repeat the checks before every flight, every day, for their entire aviation career. Over and over again, they run this same checklist.

Why? First, it is important to recall the 80/20 rule. (See "The 80/20 Rule" in Chapter 4 for a more complete explanation.) Put simply, the 80/20 rule states that often, in an engineering system, the ratio of 80/20 appears.

Tip This common ratio occurs when 80% of your problems can be addressed by focusing on the right 20%. But finishing the last 20% of the project will require the remaining 80% of effort.

The 80/20 rule is as much about a sort of engineering golden ratio as it about learning to examine solutions to a problem by assessing how much impact an individual solution offers to addressing your problem.

There are thousands of ways that an airplane can crash. Some are possible to check before a flight, and some are not. However, by checking explicitly for problems that cause a greater proportion of crashes, you can substantially reduce risk while only looking at a small subset of the overall number of accident causes. Resources are never unlimited, whether that is time, money, or expertise. When you only have time to check 20 components, you **want to be checking the right 20 components** that prevent the most possible points of failure.

And this is what the preflight checklist is designed to do. Because of the wide use of checklists in aviation, airplane disasters in the West tend to be caused by outlier situations that are hard or impossible to screen out before they happen—rare weather phenomena, acute mechanical component failure, acts of terrorism—and not by the more detectable, common failures that plagued aviation in the early years of powered flight.

A checklist thrives in situations where the 80/20 rule thrives. The goal of the checklist is simple: improve the stability of a system by checking the most common detectable causes of failure frequently.

Checklists are widely used in commercial aviation and the military, and are becoming more widely used in hospitals, where they are showing early but dramatic results in improving care.[1] The checklist has utility for project management in software and web design as well.

Here are a few ways you can use checklists in your own projects:

A sanity health checklist: this is a set of checks that assesses the health of a web application, looking at common causes of failure on the entire stack, from the server or operating system level to the application level. Items might include the following:

- Does the server have enough free disk space?
- Are there any security patches for the operating system pending installation?
- Does a port scan reveal any unexpected open ports (indicating a firewall failure)?
- In the past 24 hours, have there been any log messages of concern?
- Did the last backup succeed?
- Is e-mail successfully sending from the server?

This checklist touches upon the common areas where an application can fail, such as dependent component failure (e-mail, backups, firewall) or operating system problems (lack of disk space from runaway log files, missing patches, error log entries).

A patch checklist: these are the steps that outline the process of applying a patch to a live production site. Steps might include

- E-mailing the client to alert them the patch has started
- Putting the application into offline mode for the patch
- Making a manual backup of the database and code before the patch
- A few specific tests to run on different parts of the application to validate the patch is not causing major issues (could be the separate upgrade checklist mentioned next)
- E-mailing the client to alert them the patch is complete

An upgrade checklist: this is a series of checks on the most fragile parts of the application that you run after you patch new features or issue fixes into the production system. It is a form of a testing checklist that your developer should conduct as the last step in the patch process.

---

[1] See reading list item for "The Checklist" in the Appendix.

A testing checklist: this is a guide for those doing quality assurance testing on your application. See "Creating a Testing Checklist" in Chapter 9 for more information.

A launch checklist: this is a list of important launch-time configuration adjustments to apply to ensure a smooth, professional launch of a project. See "The Launch Checklist" in Chapter 9 for details.

Here are some general tips for creating checklists:

- When creating a new checklist, start from the last one you prepared for another project. You will not keep every item you had, but it will be a good starting point.
- Ask different team members what they think are the most likely three or four points of failure.
- When a problem occurs that your checklist did not catch, take a moment to consider if there is a check that can be added while keeping the checklist efficient.
- Think back to the major problems you have had with other applications in the past. There are likely good checks in these painful memories.
- Parts of your system that rely on third-party components are likely to be fragile (**by design; if you do not control it, you cannot trust it**). Check those.

Investing a small amount of time to create and use an efficient, targeted checklist will help prevent major system problems that might otherwise consume a far greater amount of your already scarce resources.

Don't Avoid the Pain; Go Toward It

Let's talk about the no-win-scenario (NWS) bug. You know this bug. You have no time left in the budget to troubleshoot this issue. The programmers insist there is no quick option, it will just take time. Meaning hours. Hours that are no longer available in the project budget. So the bug report sits in your queue as you are hamstrung by indecision. With no good choice to make, who wants to commit to the least bad option?

We struggle with the NWS bugs, often obsessing that there must be a clever, time-beating solution to the issue. But there is not. If you have great programmers around you and your initial questions and discussion did not produce any insight, then there likely isn't any to be found.

Just accept that the least bad option is the best option, make a decision, and move on. Do not ignore the issue. If you do, it will start to affect new modules developed in your application. Your programmers will (naturally) forget the intricacies of the issue, and so will you. You will need more time later to relearn the issue.

Open decisions in your queue are a drag on your own morale, as you can feel their burden and feel your brain nagging at you to make a decision.

Do not avoid the pain. If you have pain right there in front of you, it should be an indicator to move toward a decision. You should want to be rid of the pain by dealing with it, embracing it, and moving forward. Do not ignore it. A little pain now saves you a lot of pain later.

Keeping Documentation

Documentation is hard—mostly because very few people enjoy writing down what they are doing.

There are several kinds of documentation that you will need to ensure the success of your project. Most projects that are $100K or higher will need each of these types of documentation.

The key here is to ensure that reliable systems are in place to track the system documentation. As we review each type of documentation that you need for a successful project, we will offer our hands-on observations about some of our favorite systems for tracking these changes.

Documenting Code

When a developer writes custom code, he needs to add comments throughout explaining what he is doing. This makes it significantly easier for someone (including the same developer) to revisit the code later and make changes. It's tempting to think that you will never need to revise your custom code, but 90% of the time, you would be wrong. Here is an example of some simple commenting that you would expect to see in a developer's code:

```
/**
 * AJAX callback function. Returns the state after one step or
initialization
 */
```

This kind of documentation should always appear in your development files, inline with the code. Many developers provide very few comments on their code, or none at all, unless they know that someone is reviewing the code. The best way to ensure that your code is well-commented is to have regular code reviews where a technical project manager or another developer reads through the code and make recommendations.

Recommendation: *perform monthly code reviews to ensure that developer code is well-commented.*

Documenting the System Architecture

The system architecture is typically developed early in the project. If you have followed our advice, you will most likely have a technical specification that outlines the system architecture. However, if you do not have this, you need to capture the relevant details so that developers understand the full scope of the system and so that when you come back to the project later, you can remember the specifics.

Sometimes the simplest way to do this is to create a graphic with a visual representation of how the different parts of the system work together. This does not have to be highly technical, but it should convey at a glance how the system operates. See Figure 8-1 for an example.

Recommendation: *document the system architecture in the technical specification, or in a separate graphical document.*

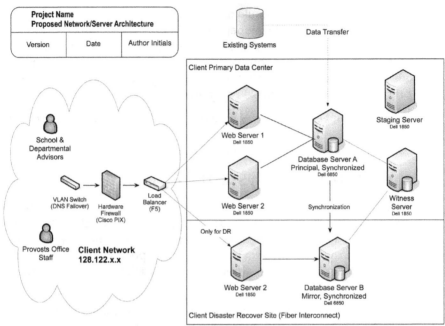

Figure 8-1. A system architecture for a cluster to power a widely-used web application.

Documenting System Administration Settings

Team members can waste a lot of time trying to find usernames, passwords, and other system administration settings. If there is no centralized location to store this information, individual team members will begin keeping "cheat sheets" with the information on a piece of paper in their desk or in a file on their computer. Not only is this not secure, but it also complicates changing settings or passwords.

Wikis are an excellent way to store system administration information. A *wiki* is a series of shared web pages. Each change is tracked, so it is easy to see what information has changed. Individual team members can be granted access to view or edit pages, based on their needs. When you have configuration changes—for example, if you create a new development site—you simply add the details to the wiki. All team members who need access can then access the wiki to obtain this information.

Figure 8-2 shows a screenshot of the template we use for client pages on the Urban Insight wiki.

Client Information

```
  Client name        : Spring Street Partners (fictional client)
  Client account     : 12345
  Client passphrase  : "The weather is cold in Paris."

  Client contacts
  Name               : Alan Abrahamson
  Telephone          : 555-555-5555
  Email              : alan@springstreetpartners.com

  UI contacts
  Project manager    : Bob P. Manager
  Support            : Joe Support, Delyte Support
```

Emergency Event Response

```
  1. Determine if server or domain is down
  2. Check to see if site is being served from the primary or backup server.
  3. Notify Urban Insight project manager.
  4. If we need to trigger the failover, execute steps for triggering it.
  5. If site might be down more than 1 hour, turn off db replication process.
  6. Notify Client contact and provide a touch-back time (less than 1 hour)
  7. Etc.
```

production.clientdomain.com (Web1)

```
  Purpose            : Production Environment (Primary)
  Public IP Address  : xxx.xxx.xxx.xxx
  NAT IP Address     : xxx.xxx.xxx.xxx
  Server             : web1.clientdomain.com (WEB1)

  Admin interface    : Admin interface
  username           : Admin username
  password           : Admin password

  FTP username       : FTP username
  FTP password       : FTP password

  Database           : database_db
  Database username  : database_usr
  Database password  : Database password

  SVN                : SVN path/credentials

  Etc.
```

Client Accounts

```
  Twitter
  Consumer Key       : Consumer Key
  Consumer Secret    : Consumer Secret
  OAuth Callback     : OAuth Callback

  Google Analytics
  username           : GA Username
  password           : GA Password

  Etc.
```

Quality Assurance Checklist

- Action 1: Load home page, confirm it looks correct.
- Action 2: Load the following key pages
  - Page 1: http://www.domain.com/page1
  - Page 2: http://www.domain.com/page2
    - Perform search on any author name
  - Load 5 other random pages.
- Action 3: Login to site as an editor.
- Etc.

Figure 8-2. A screenshot of a sample wiki page based on a fictional client, with all confidential information removed.

Recommendation: *track system administration details using a wiki.*

Documenting Changes over Time

Most successful web applications change over time as the application is refined and upgraded and as new features are added. Documenting the changes that occur over the life a system is one of the most challenging aspects of documentation.

For example, say you finish a modest project and have the developer deploy the changes to the production server. The correct code is launched, and the project is successful. Six months later, you ask another developer to make some modest refinements requested by the client. However, unbeknownst to the current developer, the initial developer made some changes on production that he failed to make on the local development copy. The programmer making refinements is working on the development copy of the application, not production, and when she pushes her refinements they will inadvertently overwrite the working code that's already there.

Version control is an elegant solution this problem. Changes to code are usually identified by a number or letter code, termed the "revision." For example, an initial set of files is "revision 1." When the first change is made, the resulting set is "revision 2," and so on. Each revision is associated with a timestamp and the person making the change. Revisions can be compared, restored, and with some types of files, merged. Version control makes it possible to see previous changes made to a file, and also to view the comments that the developer provided when committing the change.

Use Version Control

A version control system provides a system for your development team to track the changes to the source code of your project over time. A great version control system can provide a reference for every past version of a file (so nothing is lost), and keep a record of every code change. This can be helpful to understand what the thinking was when an engineer made a change.

Figure 8-3 shows the note left by a developer when he completed work on a routine to show receipts.

Figure 8-3. A log entry from a single code submission from a developer in Beanstalk

Case Tracking

Tracking individual requests for changes on a system is an important aspect of documentation. Often, tracking these changes goes hand-in-hand with the code changes that you will track in a version control system. Let's use the word *case* to refer to a specific and definable set of requested changes to a system. For example, say that your client asks you to modify your system to include a new screen that tracks changes in addresses over time.

If you were using a case tracking system, you would use the system to create a case, which would be assigned a number—say Case #1. Any communication about this particular request would be stored in the case tracking system so that you have a repository where all communications about this request are stored. For example, if you and your client discussed the specifications in an e-mail, you might send a copy of the e-mail to your case tracking system, so that e-mail becomes part of the permanent record of discussion. When you finally decide what to develop, your wireframes would be uploaded and attached to the case. When you are ready to begin development, you might create subcases—for example, Case #2 for development of the interface and Case #3 for testing. Both of these cases would be related to Case #1, so you could later identify the work that was performed.

Case tracking systems also can record the amount of time involved on a project and help you to plan your schedule based on available development capacity. Figure 8-4 shows the task view screen of an issue tracker that details a feature for a public web site.

Recommendation: *use a case tracking system to document requests and changes over time. (See the Appendix for suggestions.)*

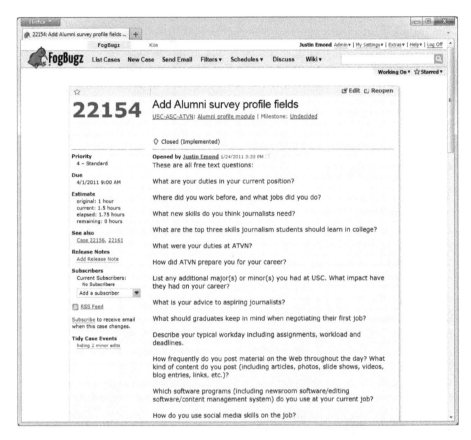

Figure 8-4. The ticket view screen in FogBugz, a popular issue tracking system

The Weekly Developer Meeting

The relationship between a project manager and a developer is much like that of a parent and a teenager: there is very little you can do as a parent to change what a teenager thinks or does. Your job is to try and nudge them in a slightly different direction when they are careening headlong off a cliff edge. (This in no way means to disparage programmers. It is programmers—not project managers—who make a great project great. However, in our experience, programmers tend not to take the big picture into consideration, but focus instead on the immediate problem at hand.)

Micromanagement is an ineffective project management technique for a variety of reasons:

- People will be frustrated that you do not trust their abilities.
- You do not like working under a micromanager, so why would anyone else?
- It takes too much time. Your time is at a premium, so spend it where it will have the most positive impact on the project.
- If a team member really needs constant supervision to be effective, you have a personnel issue, not a management issue.

The key is to maintain oversight and control of your team, but give them enough breathing room. We recommend a one-on-one weekly meeting.

The weekly meeting can be short, maybe 30 minutes. In this meeting, you have three main goals:

- Review the status of every outstanding project.
- Set a Clear priority order for what needs to get done this week.
- Discuss any complex tasks that would benefit from planning discussion.

When you review the **status of every ongoing project**, you can see if the developer has run into any issues that are making the task more complex or are requiring more time than expected. Focus on these hiccups in your meeting and be determined to find solutions.

Set a **clear priority order**, making it clear to the developer what you need accomplished over the coming week. This is also your main tool to manage the schedules of your various promises to clients about when tasks will be complete. Limit this to just two or three tasks. Anything more just will not be possible in a week (because something always unexpected happens with a client).

Lastly, use the weekly meeting to **review any complex tasks** that the developer will work on that week. This is a good time to do a "gut check" and see how the developer might approach the task. Most of the time their programmer instincts will serve them well, but it is important to make sure you know the general approach they are taking. Sometimes, you can identify and remove any mitigating factors they might not be aware of, and steer their work in a different direction.

Monday is a great day to have the weekly meeting. Team members will be fresh from a restful weekend and you can frame the week as a distinct unit.

Once you lose the developer for a weekend of fun, they will not remember what they were talking about the week before.

Finally, there are two additional benefits to a weekly one-on-one meeting. First, this is a setting that encourages frank feedback because others are not watching. And second, taking the time to meet individually helps make team members feel valued.[2]

Wrapping Up

In this chapter we looked at how to manage the development process, keep the client updated, and use checklists to ensure consistent quality. As development winds down, you will need to begin to validate your project with testing.

No one really likes testing, but it's vital to ensuring that you produce a high-quality product. Bugs in software are not a reflection of mistakes or poor programming skills. They are a reflection of the reality that technology is a hard, complicated game that involves subtle interactions with many independent systems (such as other code modules you have written, third-party applications you integrate with, and hardware you run on). Software bugs indicate a failure of project management, not of development.

Naturally, the next chapter focuses on testing. We cover the different kinds of testing that a project can involve, how to write a testing checklist (which gets your client to do some of testing work for you), and how to manage a client beta test. We wrap up with guidance on how to conduct useful but easy usability tests and share a war story about a beta test gone horribly wrong.

---

[2] Although a discussion of what motivates people is beyond the scope of this book, most modern research confirms that having a sense of worth and accomplishment in one's work is more motivating than money.

Quality Assurance and Testing

The Developer Who Refused to Test

Cathy is a programmer for a five-person web development firm. She enjoys her work, although she feels that often there is too little time allocated for her to complete her work.

Cathy has noticed in the past several months that the company's lead developer has been asking her to come up with estimates for specific tasks, and then includes another 20% of her time for "testing." Cathy is often optimistic about writing code—it is fun, after all—and does not always guess the appropriate amount of time a task will take.

This week Cathy estimated it would take her 3 days to develop a new feature for an existing web application. The lead developer had allocated 4 days, plus a day for testing, for a total of 5 days. Cathy felt sure that she would have no problem finishing the work in that length of time.

The project started off well, and Cathy finished the first half in just a day. She knew that she should do some testing before moving on, but Cathy—like most developers—despises testing, although she recognizes that it must be done. The next morning, she decides to move into the second half of the task now and do the testing later. While working on the second half—which is a little more complex than she had expected—she identifies a few issues in the original application that are causing problems for her. She invests a few hours fixing the original application, which quickly turns into a full day of work because she has to fully understand the original web application. She gets bogged down for still another day before giving up on trying to fix the original problem. She is now in her fourth day of work and struggling to finish the second half of the task. The lead developer checks in midway through the fourth day to see how things are progressing. Cathy is confident she will be able to finish the work soon, so she reports no problems.

Sure enough, Cathy finishes the second component around the middle of the fifth day. Cathy feels that she has done a great job, and for the first time in her work pushes the code onto a staging server, where she can begin testing. Of course, the new module breaks as soon as it hits the development server, and it takes until the end of the day to fix the code so it works on the staging server. By the time she is ready to leave work, she quickly browses through the application to make sure all the pages are working, then resolves the case for her boss to review and heads out for a well-deserved beer.

Midway into her second beer, she gets a text message from the lead developer asking her to check her e-mail. She sees a flood of bug reports filed by the lead developer. Each bug report shows an increasing level of frustration. Sure, she had not exactly tested each *field* in her application, but anyone can see that she finished building it. Little bugs in field display and validation, or minor issues with workflow are easy to fix. She cannot understand at all when the lead developer sends her a visibly upset e-mail asking her to come in this weekend to finish development.

This chapter explains how to create a realistic testing plan and perform testing early in the development process, with an eye on preventing episodes like the one we just described.

About Testing

Testing is vital for any project you manage. Every project needs some kind of testing, careful review, and quality assurance (QA). Typically, you will have several phases of testing:

- **Developer testing**: when a developer completes a task, he should conduct his own testing to confirm it is working.
- **Project manager review**: when a developer reports a task is complete, the project manager should review the feature for completeness and do some testing.

- **QA testing**: this is when a person runs through a module or the entire application against your testing checklist (see "Creating a Testing Checklist" later in this chapter).
- **Beta testing**: when testing internally is complete, the client can beta test the project before launch (see "How to Manage a Beta Test with a Client" later in this chapter for some great tips).

Developer and project manager testing happen throughout the development process as different modules and features of the project are completed. This is also the perfect time for the project manager to be appending the latest feature's components to a growing testing checklist. Putting this checklist together a piece at a time helps ensure that nothing is left out, making the QA testing phase much easier.

Phases of QA testing tend to occur at the end of the project, before beta testing and before launch. A QA test is also a good time to get outsider feedback on the project. For consulting engagement projects, the QA tester is likely not familiar with the project yet, which is good. Their perspective will be very different from yours and your development team's, so the questions they ask or the problems they have will often be telling. **Listen closely to what they do, what they cannot do, what they ask about, and what confuses them**. Listen less to what they say.

Your Software Is Only as Good as Your Testing

In the process of designing and managing the development of several web-based applications, we have come to learn a critical lesson in software development (which many others in the software industry likely already know):

Your software is only as good as the testing you perform.

Take a real example.

Justin worked on a team that recently released a web-based chat tool. Powered by jQuery, the tool enables college and university admissions recruiters to easily host web chats for talking with prospective students.

The Bug

The application worked great during beta testing, until more than 20 chatters joined a room. Then odd things started to happen: chatters were dropped from the room, some could not join the room at all, and others just got an endless "connection waiting" message when trying to load the room URL.

But none of these issues happened consistently, only intermittently. We could not regularly reproduce the issue, so it was impossible to fix. We focused on other bugs.

A few weeks went by and we still had no luck in finding the cause of the issue. Then we decided to really test out the application by hosting a high-profile chat where we expected more than 75 participants.

What a difference a little pressure makes. We were forced to take a different approach to debugging the issue. So we ran a more complex test on the bug and dug a bit into how Apache, a LAMP application, works. Eventually, we found the source of the bug, fixed the issue, and felt confident that the application would support 80 chatters in one room.

Test, Debug, Refine, and Repeat

If we had not been forced to test the application harder, the true source of the bug would never have been identified, the software would not scale as well as we needed it to, and (worst of all) **customers would have had problems with our software**.

Your software will not get better on its own; you have to force it to become better with great developers, useful features, and—most of all—hard testing. Over and over again. From different angles and vectors. From different computers, networks, browsers, operating systems, locations, monitors, and processors.

This is not a new revelation, but it is an important one.

Creating a Testing Checklist

Creating testing checklists is actually pretty simple. Start by opening up your application to the home screen. For each screen, try to **imagine all of the things a user can do and all of the ways a user can mess things up**. You want to test for both.

> **Tip** In essence, your testing checklist is a just a to-do list that should force the tester eventually to visit every part of your application. **Your ultimate goal is to point out all of the things that need testing and any special cases**.

For example, here are some real entries from a web content management project:

- Use the "forgot password" link and confirm you can login and reset your password.
- In the attendees listing table, sort by various columns and confirm the sorting works.
- Edit a page and confirm editing works.
- Upload and add an attachment to a content page.
- Filter the events management listing screen by various criteria and verify they work.
- View the user home page and verify all upcoming events are listed.

Generally, you want to balance specificity—trying to touch upon every feature of the application—with brevity. You should not need to specify exactly how to test each feature. For example, you should not need to tell a QA tester what kinds of values to use in a text search box to see if there are encoding issues with the form. (If you do need to mention this, you have an inexperienced tester.)

In addition to touching upon each part of the application, be sure to mention in the testing checklist any non-obvious relationships between actions in one section that should impact another section. These are special cases that you want to call out.

For example, imagine you have a filter feature on a search screen. You will have a testing checklist item like, "Perform a variety of different filters with various criteria, and verify the results are consistent with the criteria." If the system logs these filters and shows them in the log screen of the application, you should mention in your testing document not only the steps to access and use the log screen, but also specifically that verification is needed to confirm that the tester's earlier filter activities are logged here.

Finally, as you become more experienced, you will find there is a (growing) set of actions that tend to be problematic and need to be checked for in the kinds of projects you tend to manage. You do not need to write these down, as a moment spent thinking of past projects should recall these.

Here are a few examples from web-based content management systems:

- Uploading files from a client PC to the system
- Embedding media, like video from YouTube or Blip.tv
- Encoding and escaping issues with HTML1
- Character encoding issues with non-Latin alphabets
- Pasting content from a Microsoft Word document

Here are few additional tips for creating testing checklists:

- Think about **problems from similar past projects**. Many of these are likely to happen again, so test for them.
- When you start a project, **start a blank testing checklist** somewhere. A text file, a Word document, your internal wiki documentation; it does not matter where. What is important is that it is written down somewhere. During development—as you review a completed module, section, or feature—you now have a handy place to quickly jot down items that need to be tested, before you forget about them.
- Do not get lost in the testing instruction details. Touch upon every feature, but let the testers do their jobs.
- In the testing document, be clear whether the tester needs to check with a programmer or developer before testing an external-facing component (like an e-mail system).
- When considering a checklist item to test a component, ignore any thought of "this is too obvious to mention." **Something obvious to you is not necessarily obvious to others**.
- Do not forget to test for size. If your system has a search feature and you only have ten sample rows in the database, then be sure to have a step that includes testing a search with 10,000 rows. How large? Imagine how much data the client will accumulate using your application over the next 5 years. Multiply that by ten and you have your dataset size.

---

[1] Proper encoding is necessary to protect against cross-site scripting attacks, which are an important security vulnerability.

Testing Checklist Format

The testing document format can be very simple:

- It should have a brief introduction section to state the critical details, such as where to log in to start testing and a two- to three-sentence explanation of the system.
- It should have any testing notes, such as instructions to alert a developer before they begin testing, or any special considerations.
- The testing checklist can be in the form of a table, with three columns:

  - Column 1 should be a sequential number. It is helpful to have a way to reference specific items in a long list.
  - Column 2 should be the testing checklist item, the task at hand.
  - Column 3 should be a small blank box for either checking off the task or including a reference to an issue/case/ticket number if a bug report was filed.

If the testing checklist is long, you can use rows to break up sections, with just a section name in the row. The format of this document is not critical, but a small amount of effort up front means that later in the project, during beta testing, you can share this document with the client to assist them in testing the application thoroughly (a frequent challenge for even the best clients). Figure 9-1 presents a sample testing checklist.

37.	Create several discussion forums and confirm postings work as expected.	
38.	Log in as a user of the role "student contributor" and create several blog posts. Confirm you can publish them and they appear in the blog home page for anonymous visitors.	
	Zeitgeist Dashboard	
39.	Identify a story in the Zeitgeist Dashboard "Most talked about stories" section that is not at the top, add enough comments to the story to make it move up a position and reload the dashboard to confirm this is reflected.	
40.	Pick a term not in the "Top Searches" box and search for it 10 times. Confirm the term now appears on this box.	
41.	Click on several random tag, story and Twitter links and confirm everything loads as expected.	
42.	Confirm each chart loads without error.	
43.	Log in and out of the site as several different users and confirm "Recently logged in users" reflects this activity.	
	Rich Media	
44.	Create a Google Map, complete with custom shapes, position and zoom, and embed it into a node. Create two additional nodes with two additional (different) maps.	
45.	Create several wiki pages. Verify wiki syntax (Creole style) works (see http://www.wikicreole.org/wiki/EditPageHelp)	
46.	Create several stories and verify each of the formatting options available in the editor for the BODY field are preserved when the node is saved and viewed.	
	Editorial Control Panel	
47.	Using the stories you have created so far, setup a blank storyboard, populate every box and make the storyboard live on the home page. Verify home page formatting, links and media are correct.	
48.	Setup a new storyboard with a different template and complete the task described in the previous step. Set this as a new, live section home page.	
49.	Setup a new storyboard with a different template and complete the task described in the previous step. Set this as a new, live section home page.	
50.	Duplicate an existing template to create a new one, change three boxes and post live. Confirm changes are set.	
51.	Set a RANK of 1 on several recent stories you added. Create a new blank storyboard and use the auto-populate feature. Confirm all places stories are recent, and ones ranked 1 appear first.	
	Permissions Testing	
52.	Log in as a site editor and confirm you can only access ECP, user management and blocks.	
53.	As a site editor verify you cannot access any other Drupal admin functions.	
54.	Verify that anonymous cannot register on the site.	
55.	Log in as a contributor and confirm you cannot publish nodes and cannot access any Drupal administration page.	

Figure 9-1. A testing checklist for NeonTommy.com

How to Manage a Beta Test with a Client

Eventually, you will show your project to the client and conduct some beta testing. A successful beta testing phase will reveal context-specific bugs that are obvious only to those intimate with the workflow and data in question, as well as obscure bugs that require several conditions to exist in parallel to appear.

A great way to start your beta testing is with a kickoff training meeting where you demo the application to the client team and discuss how beta testing will work. When introducing beta testing to the client, it is important to discuss a few things:

- Recap where the project is in the schedule and what will be the next steps after beta testing is complete.
- State the goals of beta testing plainly: find issues we are not aware of, and fix them.
- If a user breaks the application, the application is at fault, not the user. The client cannot damage anything permanently. Breaking the system is a good thing.
- A beta system has been tested and refined, but there are likely to be issues. That is why we are beta testing.
- Make it clear to the client that more time spent beta testing now will reduce the investment needed to further refine the application after launch, when those refinements will not be in scope.
- Explain that any data entered in the beta system will be wiped and reset.

There are a variety of challenges to client beta testing that often make it hard to capture meaningful feedback:

- Most clients will only spend a trivial amount of time testing. A **lack of client engagement** is likely to be your biggest challenge.
- Clients find it discouraging that because the beta system will be wiped, any work they do seems to be a wasted effort.
- Clients may not know how to test or what to do with the application.

Here are some tips to improve the chance of success:

- Have the beta run on **production hardware with real data**. You will wipe the data after testing (be clear about this to the client), but real data makes the application more meaningful to the client, which in turn should make their feedback more meaningful.

- Be up front with the client and tell them that most beta testing fails because a lack of client engagement.
- Identify a good candidate on the client team to be the internal evangelist. An internal evangelist is a computer-literate power user (though not a programmer or technical expert) who is both likely to be a user of the application and happy to help people on his or her team use it. Doing some one-on-one training with the evangelist can ease the amount of questions you get during testing and empower this user to become the office expert.
- Give homework.

Tip Identifying a strong internal evangelist on your client's team is a great way to empower a member of your client's team to help with training and project acceptance.

Homework Is for the Little People

While homework can be a reviled tool for educating young minds, it can be a great method to increase client engagement and force real testing to occur in the beta review period. Beta testing homework can be just a list of specific tasks that need to be completed.

For example, here are a few homework items for a back-end university admissions system:

- Create a report of all students who meet the criteria for three different academic scholarships, for review by the scholarship committee.
- Capture the data needed for a report you regularly turn in to your superior.
- Fully prepare the admissions letters for five random students. Complete the process as you would normally: print the letter, get it signed, and seal it in the real envelopes you use.

Stress the following when assigning the beta testing homework to the client: if you complete each of these tasks, the beta test will be successful. If you do not, it is likely to fail.

The goals should be clear, but also should encourage the real workflow to be carried out from start to finish, even if that means leaving the application itself. You want to capture these "edge" conditions. (In the above example, the third goal helps catch any problems with the aligning text in window-pane envelopes.)

You can create these goals by reviewing your testing checklist and picturing how the various checklist items relate to specific workflows that you can call out as homework tasks.

Horror Story: Who Is the Real Client?

An easy way to turn a bad situation into a positive one is to make it a teachable moment. A *teachable moment* is an opportunity to reflect on an incident and extract a valuable lesson. And so it was with our project, the topic of our horror story.

The project started off well enough. The exploration meeting (see "Project Kickoff" in Chapter 3) was attended by our project sponsor (the IT manager) and a group of higher-level stakeholders. There were no actual users of the application at this meeting. At the time, this seemed normal; in hindsight, this should have been the first indication of a problem.

The initial requirements gathering meeting was attended by our project sponsor and a group of lower-level stakeholders than the initial meeting. This group was more opinionated and outspoken than the group at the initial meeting and provided more specific details on how the system should work. This is a generally a great sign because it usually denotes understanding of the problem. We had our users. . . . or so we thought.

A new group of people was asked to attend the follow-up requirements gathering meetings, where we reviewed and refined the draft requirements document. They attended these meetings along with their supervisors, but were not outspoken and did not provide much feedback. It was not immediately clear, but these new folks had never participated in a project development process before and had likely never seen anything resembling a requirements document. Although it was clear they were a sharp bunch, they were essentially interns at the organization, so we assumed they were not the real stakeholders.

We entered the development phase of the project and happily developed the application over the next several months. Then it came time to schedule the beta test. That was when the problems started.

Based on our explanation of what a beta test is, the client invited back the entire group of interns that were represented by their leadership in the earlier requirements meetings. Unbeknownst to us, the leadership of this group had changed during development, so we were dealing with a leadership team that had not attended the earlier requirements gathering meetings and had not been involved with the entire process.

The feedback was significant during the beta kickoff meeting, and the questions and changes kept coming in during the testing process. Although we responded as quickly and completely as possible to the client, the questions kept coming. We made loads of refinements to the system and answered hundreds of questions by e-mail on functionality in the first week of testing alone. The problems continued after beta testing. Because of all of these challenges, our initial launch attempt was aborted and rescheduled for a week later.

Although the project launched with only a slight delay and is now in successful production use, it was a challenging process toward the end of the project. And challenges at the end of a project are even more frustrating because at that point, your energy level is lower and you just want to be finished.

Though the client never directed frustration toward us, the tone of the e-mails made it clear that the intern team was frustrated at the "surprises" in how the application worked and at not being involved during the decision-making process. You have probably seen this before in your own work: the group felt like this "thing" had been dropped on them by the higher-ups. The issue here was not that something was forced onto this group, but the process by which the system was delivered.

So what went wrong with the project? The main answer is that we did not know who the real users were. At first, we thought the client sponsor was our user. When it was clear that was not the case, we thought the next group—the higher-level supervisors—were our real users. Not until beta testing did it become clear that the real users were the interns who had undergone their own leadership change during the course of development. We entered development with the wrong users in mind!

Only in beta testing—with a new group of interns in place actually using the application—did it become clear who the real users were. Had we focused on this group from the start of the project, the beta testing phase would have been much easier, the feedback level much lower, the number of refinements needed reduced, and the training-based questions fewer.

We learned a few important takeaways from this experience:

- Explicitly ask—even when you are certain you are correct—**who the actual users are**. If there is some resistance from the client to bring these users to table, then find out why immediately. You need this group involved from the start.
- Ask the client to help you identify who is likely to become the **internal client expert** on the forthcoming application. This is likely someone to whom members of the client's team go for help and guidance. Ensuring this person feels involved and empowered and well-trained before the rest of the team will help reduce the "surprises" during beta testing and launch.
- If we had known the interns were the actual user base and were told of the leadership change (it was planned), it may have been possible to have the future team leader attend the earlier requirements meetings prior to her leaving that position.

Usability Testing

The goal of usability testing is to make software easier to use by making it a more intuitive experience. From the perspective of a project budget, the entire goal of a usability test is **to identify issues in the interaction of your application with people that will be less expensive to fix the earlier they are caught**.

The return on investment of usability testing is well-documented. Commerce-driven projects that have never done any usability testing can expect to double conversion rates and other key revenue-centric business metrics by applying the results of the first test.[2]

For a consulting-driven process, the savings are real, too. If you catch a navigation issue during the screen prototyping phase, it takes a few minutes for that navigation to be changed in the mock-ups. When the application is fully built, it will take a developer more time to fix, test, and deploy modifications to the navigation. **Remember the rule of project avoidance**: the later a change is made, the more expensive it becomes to complete.

---

[2] Jakob Nielsen, "Return on Investment for Usability," www.useit.com/alertbox/roi-first-study.html, January 7, 2003.

The great news about usability testing is that it does not take much time, you do not need formal training,[3] and you do not need expensive equipment. Research even shows that you can find out most usability problems with as few as five users.[4]

So What Do You Test?

Your usability test should ask users to complete the kind of tasks users would normally do when using your application. If you have an information-driven site, this might include asking users to find out specific facts that you built your site to disseminate. If you have an e-commerce site, focus your tests on product search, comparison, and purchase. If you are building a web application, focus on the workflow goals you are attempting to streamline in your software.

Watching a real user get stuck, go the wrong way, or misunderstand your interface is very insightful. Indeed, having your development team watch this process is a great way to remind the programmers that humans are eventually going to use this thing you are building.

The different kinds of usability tests available to you are defined by where in the project you would normally use them:

- **Paper prototyping**. In paper prototyping, you take a piece of paper and quickly draw up how a page in your application might look. You can use cutouts for navigation elements or just draw them with a black marker. It does not matter. Grab someone in the office who is not working on the project, drop the paper in front of them, and watch what they do as you ask questions like, "Using your finger, show me where you would click to do a search," or, "What do you expect to find when clicking each button?"
- **Hallway usability testing**. Coined by software blogger Joel Spolsky, this test works very well during development or the screen mock-up phase. As you complete a screen or section of the interface, grab someone walking by your office and have them try it

---

[3] Jakob Nielsen, "Anybody Can Do Usability," http://www.useit.com/alertbox/anybody-usability.html, December 21, 2009.

[4] Jakob Nielsen, "Why You Only Need to Test with 5 Users," http://www.useit.com/alertbox/20000319.html, March 19, 2000.

out. You can ask questions similar to those for paper prototyping and just watch what they do.

- **Classic usability test.** In a classic usability test, you work with an application that is more or less fully functional (a beta is fine). The most effective method is to have the user alone in an office with a computer and a list of tasks they need to complete. It is best to record the screen and the reaction of the user during this process (there are cheap software applications that can do this for you with just a webcam) and to leave the room after a brief introduction.

You can also obtain valuable insights by evaluating your interface against established usability guidelines. It is easy to find good lists of things to check if you do some simple searching. An added benefit of this process is that it can be instructive for you and your team to learn about the common traps in user interface design that are best avoided in future projects.

For your first classic usability test, start small. Set a goal to recruit and test with five users, use a simple setup (commandeer an office with a computer for a day and purchase a $20 webcam), and have a modest list of tests to conduct. Run the test, review your results, and consider your next steps.

Usability testing is very helpful for iterative design. If you only have time for one or two usability tests, then iterate. Run the first test with five users, refine your application from your findings, and conduct a follow-up test with a site that includes the refinements. This will allow you to both validate the fixes you implemented for the previously identified design flaws, and—if you successfully addressed these earlier design flaws—to identify the next major set of issues that need attention. One or two rounds of iteration will allow you to address all of the low-hanging fruit that will offer the most return on investment for your time.

There is a great amount of reading online about usability testing that goes far deeper into the topic than is appropriate here. A great place to start is Jakob Nielsen's *Alertbox* (see the reading list in the Appendix), a one-stop shop for everything you need to know to conduct successful usability tests and design amazing, intuitive, and clear interfaces. Also take a look at the reading list at the end of the book for some additional articles we think you will find especially helpful.

Do not be put off by the perceived complexity and cost. Usability testing can be a fun, cheap way to catch problems early on. **Good luck and good testing**!

Wrapping Up

Once you have completed testing and making refinements to the system, it will be time to deploy your project. By this point, your project budget is nearly depleted and the morale and energy of the team can be low, especially if you had a challenging testing period.

It will be tempting to not apply the same amount of planning rigor to deployment as you did in earlier phases of the project. Resist this urge! Regardless of the quality of the project, a client will judge the entire process negatively if the deployment isn't smooth.

In the next chapter, we look at deployment in detail. We provide real tips you can use when planning deployment, explain the importance of training, and detail a comprehensive launch checklist you can use with your team to become a deployment rock star.

We finish out the chapter by covering the often neglected but vital step of defining post-launch support.

Deployment

A Failed Deployment

Josh was ready for the project to be over. He had written many change orders and handled lots out-of-scope requests from the client. Worse, the project was behind schedule and the budget was depleted. Josh wanted to launch the web site and put this project behind him. The quicker this project became a memory, the better.

The launch involved importing a large data set and user accounts and upgrading a live, production web site. The development team had done the import once during testing. Although they had hit a few bugs, they had updated the script so that it would work better during the next import. However, due to the tight budget, they had not actually tested the new import script. Josh figured it would be a breeze and didn't worry about it. He scheduled the launch date and time with the client, met briefly with the lead programmer the day before launch to make sure everything was ready, and went to bed the night before hoping everything would go well.

When they started the launch the next morning, the situation started off poorly, and quickly got worse. Transferring several gigabytes of legacy data between the legacy network and the new server took much longer than anticipated. The data import failed during the first attempt, and the import script had to be updated and run again. This put pressure on the launch schedule for every subsequent item. Then, during the legacy user import, the system "accidentally" generated an unexpected e-mail to each user.

By the time the new site was scheduled to be live, the data import had yet to be completed and users were calling the client to ask about the e-mail notifications they received. An hour after the scheduled launch time, the client called off the launch and the old site was put back online. The launch failed and the client was frustrated.

Josh made a lot of mistakes here. First, and probably most damaging, is how the client will evaluate the project. Like it or not, the client will judge much of the project's success on how the launch went. A failed launch is embarrassing to you as a project manager, but it's likewise embarrassing for the client who has to answer to his superiors.

Secondly, Josh's preparations for the launch were inadequate. Launches are complex events that require planning and coordination among many parties, systems, and processes. A good launch is planned ahead of time and practiced, so the client and development team know exactly what to expect.

Josh's last mistake was failing to perform a full test of the data import. Data imports are fickle affairs that rely heavily on the network conditions between the two systems involved. The best way to ensure a smooth data import is to test the entire import process—every step, not just the actual import step—ahead of time, until you have it running smoothly.

In previous chapters we covered the steps and stages of a project in development, from idea to deliverable. Since deployments are so vital, we focus on this topic exclusively in this chapter. We provide a clear outline of how to prepare for a launch and share in detail the launch checklist we use to make sure that new sites go live smoothly.

Deployment Process and Planning

Launch day is an exciting (*an end to a bleeding budget! Yay!*) and stressful (*what do you mean you need 12 hours to run the import?*) event. With a little preparation, you can reduce the stress and increase the chances of a successful launch.

The launch event merits planning time, not only because you want it to be a success, but also because this is a time in the project when the client will be watching closely. A smooth launch builds credibility, trust, and faith. A disastrous launch is a source of frustration. (Remember: your client has to tell his or her boss why the *thing* did not go live.)

This often-used but rarely heeded advice is relevant for launch planning: plan for the worst, hope for the best. **Everyone likes a secretly prepared optimist**. No matter the planning, something bad *will happen* on launch day. The more of these potential "gotchas" you eliminate well in advance of the launch, the more time you have to address the hiccups when time is tight.

Here are some pointers for improving launch:

Pointer #1: Create a Launch-day Checklist

Not to be confused with the web site launch checklist we outline later, a launch-day checklist is really a step-by-step schedule of what needs to happen during the actual launch process. You can start this early in the project, the moment you come across something that will need to happen at launch (do this no matter how distant launch may seem or how simple the task might be). Once you have this document, it will be easy for you to add items to it over time.

This does not need to be a long formal document. It should be a simple list of concise steps for launch. Consider adding the initials of the team member responsible for completing the task at the end of each step. If a task requires more than one person, just pick one and assign them.

Tip Remember: a task assigned to two people will be completed by no one.

The launch-day checklist should include every discrete step needed for launch, including steps for

- Configuration changes
- Data imports
- Backups
- Code updates
- DNS changes
- Hosting changes
- Version control refinements
- E-mails to clients and team members (see "Tips for Writing E-mails" in Chapter 8)
- Scheduling new tasks for post-launch marketing
- QA testing (see Pointer #8)

Pointer #2: Double Your Estimate for the Time Needed to Launch

When telling the client how long a launch will take, be sure to double your estimate. Problems will occur; give yourself a bit of breathing room.

Pointer #3: When Possible, Perform a Soft Launch

A soft launch is when you make an application live ahead of when it will first be seen or used by a larger audience. If you are launching a new site or application and not replacing an existing tool in production use, you can likely roll out the project a day in advance of when it is advertised to be ready. This will ensure that if there is a problem, there will be time to address it. If your client is planning a marketing blitz for a new site, launch in the afternoon the day before the "marketing launch day."

Pointer #4: Be Leery of Time Estimates for Data Imports

If your launch includes a data import step, be sure to run a complete test on the import well ahead of the launch to confirm that it will run in a reasonable amount of time. Ensure that your test uses both the same amount of data and the same transmission path as the launch import will to check for network-induced delays.

Pointer #5: Meet with the Development Team Several Days Before Launch

No matter how straightforward you expect the launch to be, have a meeting with the development team that will be launching the project. Bring your draft launch-day checklist, and spend the meeting going over the steps you will use to launch the site. Ideally, this will help your team identify any potential issues you have not thought of, giving you time to plan out how to mitigate them.

Additionally, use this meeting to make clear what you expect from each team member on launch day and how you will communicate. For example, if you are launching on Sunday morning and everyone is working from home, you can agree to meet over instant messaging and invite them to a group chat.

Pointer #6: Update the Client When You Start and Complete the Launch

Be sure to send a quick note to the client when you start the launch and when you finish it. This will make them feel involved and reduce ambiguity over how the process is going.

Pointer #7: Double-Check Your Third-Party Integration

Your site likely has some dependence on third-party tools, be it a simple newsletter sign-up form or a more complex centralized authentication mechanism. Launches involve big configuration changes, so double-check that nothing needs to be updated in your project for the external integration to continue to work (like different credentials intended for production use).

Pointer #8: Test!

Once the actual launch is complete—but before you have told anyone so—you should perform testing on the site. Ideally, your launch-day checklist should have a series of quick tests that you and the team can perform on the site to check for any issues.

Here are some general tips:

- Breadth over depth: make sure you hit every major section of the application, rather than test every detail.
- If you need ideas for what to test, review your testing checklist for the project.
- Try to keep the list short (10 to 25 items).
- Ensure that each testing item can be easily validated.
- Speed up testing by dividing the checklist items throughout the launch team.

Only after you have tested the site should you feel confident about announcing the launch is complete.

Training

Training is a key step in the successful launch of a project, both because it prepares users to properly beta test the application and because users will be unaware of features they will think are missing.

Here are some tips for delivering training:

- **Have a clear training agenda.** Like a normal meeting, it is important to have a clear agenda of the topics you will cover. This has two benefits: trainees will have a sense of what to expect in the training, and you will likely remember to include topics in your agenda that you might normally gloss over.
- **Do not assume that something is obvious.** As a project manager for a web project, your own history of using, developing, and enjoying web applications means that you have a catalog of knowledge about how various interface mechanisms work. You might think the client has this knowledge, but they do not.
- **When you start the training, make it clear that questions are welcome.** The client team in your training is likely to include people who have not been on the project team. These people do not know you and are often more junior than the core client team. They need to know you are friendly and happy to answer questions or go over something again.
- **Don't show, do.** It is more helpful to a trainee to see how you do something than to hear how it's done.
- **Have the users try, too.** Showing is great, doing is better. If you have the facilities for each team member to be online, consider showing a feature and then having the client try what you just showed. You do not need to do this for every feature, but focusing on a core set will produce some good questions from the client.
- **Practice makes less bad.** Be sure to run through your training agenda before you deliver the training. You want to catch any embarrassing bugs or configuration issues that could impact training before you are in front of the client.
- **Make training the beta kickoff.** There is not much to be gained from training the users on the system without a clear goal or next step. Make the training session the kickoff for the beta testing. This way, you will follow up a training session with an immediate reason

for the client to actually use the application, helping to increase retention.

- **Take notes**. Because the training session is likely the first time you are showing the client a functioning application, be sure to capture any misconceptions in design from feedback. You will not have time to do anything with these now, but have them written down so they can be included in the post-beta wrap-up.

- **Have your materials ready.** During training you are likely to need media assets, such as images, when demoing features. Have these ready before your training and, if possible, make them relevant to the project. (For example, you can pull images from the client's web site.)

The Launch Checklist

We have already discussed the power of checklists. Used effectively, a simple, targeted checklist can be very effective in reducing errors and decreasing the likelihood of future issues in a project. A checklist is especially vital when launching a web site because the project will be evaluated in the first 5 minutes the client spends reviewing the site once it is live. For better or worse, there is a **very limited window when the impression of your work quality is formed**.

To help ensure the smooth launch of web site projects, we run this checklist against a site shortly before launch. Although not every element in our list will be appropriate for your projects, this should help you to write your own checklist.

The Web Site Launch Checklist

This Launch Checklist is not a replacement for quality assurance testing. Rather, this Launch Checklist is a final opportunity for you to ensure that you have taken care of the many important details that are sometimes overlooked in the rush to launch a web site.

- **Cross-Browser Check**
  Test the site in the three most common browsers in use[1] (double-check that your list includes the browsers you know to be in use at the client's office) and ensure the visual layout is consistent.

- **Basic or Advanced Web Accessibility Measures**
  If the project includes Section 508 accessibility compliance, make sure that the site still meets these criteria by using an automated assessment tool available on the web.

- **Forms Check**
  Fill out a form on the site (like a "contact us" form), and ensure the form submission works and the spam protection is active.

- **Graceful Degradation**
  Turn off JavaScript in your browser, click-browse through five pages, and verify that the site is still usable.

- **Print Style Sheet**
  Print the homepage and ensure that unnecessary elements are hidden (such as side navigation).

- **Install an SSL Certificate**
  If the site has any kind of login, purchase and install a valid certificate[2] and ensure the login page forces connections over SSL.

- **Domain Standardization**
  Ensure that requests without the "www" are redirected to the same page with the "www," and that by default the web server is compressing all text files (like CSS, JavaScript, and HTML pages).

- **Analytics**
  Update the analytics settings for your site to use the profile associated with the production domain name. If available in your analytics software, set up a monthly report to be e-mailed to the client.

- **Custom 404 Error Page**
  Check that the site has a nice 404 (not found) page. Search the web for "cool 404 pages" for some ideas.

---

[1] As of this writing the most common browsers are Internet Explorer (6, 7, and 8), Firefox (2 and 3), and Chrome.

[2] SSL certificates are no longer expensive. Domain verification certificates (perfectly adequate for non–e-commerce sites) are inexpensive, easily available from vendors such as GoDaddy, and register as valid in all browsers.

- **Page Titles**
  Ensure that every top-level category page has a different clear and concise page title.
- **Home Page Meta Description**
  Add a one-sentence description of the site in a META tag in the header.
- **CMS Refinements**
  It is likely you are using some kind of content management system for the site. Ensure the settings for your CMS match the requirements provided by the vendor for production web sites.
- **CMS Accounts**
  If your project uses a content management system, ensure that an account for the client has been created and that the permissions assigned to that account are sufficient for all client needs, but do not include super-user level access.
- **Automated Site Link Check**
  Use the W3C Link Checker tool to quickly identify and fix any dead links.
- **Broadcast E-mail Integration**
  If your project includes integration with a third-party e-mail system, verify that the subscription form correctly subscribes people to the desired mailing list, the list is sensibly named, and the subscribe and unsubscribe pages are branded with the client's logo.
- **Favicon**
  Ensure the web browser favicon is loading correctly.
- **QA Review**
  Being involved with a project for a long time often blinds you to problems that might be present. Ask a team member who did not work on the project to spend 30 minutes performing some basic tests of the site and provide feedback on possible bugs and sections that do not make sense.
- **Review Proposal, Amendments, Requirements**
  Double-check the project proposal and requirements documents to ensure that all site components have been addressed.
- **Send Launch E-mail**
  Usually, the launch of a site will trigger a new phase in the project (such as a 30-day post-launch support window). Send a friendly note to

*the client congratulating them on the launch, alerting them the site is
officially active, and documenting that support has begun.*

- **Send a Gift!**
  *The client has worked hard over the past several months to help you
  launch the site. Commemorate their achievement by sending a gift
  basket.*

- **Marketing**
  *Consider mentioning the project launch on the company blog, the
  company Twitter account, to colleagues that might be interested in the
  project, and as an article or case study in the articles section on your
  site.*

The characteristics of your own projects will define what kind of launch
checklist is most appropriate, but do take the time to create and document
one. The benefits will become quickly apparent.

The Importance of Defining Post-Launch Support

It is a truth universally acknowledged that a project, once launched, must be
in want of a set of a bug fixes. Creating software is hard, complicated work.
Though you and your team worked diligently to ensure a product of high
quality, there will always be issues that you cannot identify during testing,
refinement, and launch.

Less experienced clients may expect you to support the software you
created indefinitely, but this is impractical for all involved. It is fair that the
time your team spends making refinements is compensated, and post-launch
support cannot go on forever. However, you want to be sure to balance
protection of your budget with showing that you are dedicated to the successful launch of the project.

If you are not up front about how post-launch support will work, then the
client will be left with only their own expectations to guide their behavior.
Those expectations will inevitably be at odds with your own.

The best way to achieve this is to define well ahead of time a specific cut-off
time for post-launch support. You can and should put this in your scope of
work. You can also clearly state how post-launch support will work when
you are sending an e-mail update to the client about the upcoming launch.

Be explicit. Here is an example:

Hi Team,

I wanted to write to give you an update on the launch schedule.

The web site launch will kick off a 30-day support window. We will address any issues reported during the 30 days after launch under the original scope of work. Any issues identified after the support window will be addressed on a time-and-materials basis or under a separate support plan (if you prefer to set one up).

Kindly let me know if you have any questions, concerns, or wish to discuss further. I'm happy to set up a conference call if you like. Just let me know.

Thanks,

{call sign}

By clearly stating how the process will work, there should not be any frustrations or surprises when, a month after launch, support is a new cost.

Wrapping Up

Hopefully this chapter will help guide you through a successful deployment for your project. A properly planned and tested launch will ensure a positive capstone to what we expect was an otherwise successful project, a happy client, and a satisfied project team. However, launching is not the end.

An important client expectation to manage is how the project will be managed and supported by your team after launch. You can't support a project forever under the existing scope that defined the creation of the project, but you can ease the transition by making it clear how support will work.

In the next chapter, we cover the topic of post-launch support in detail. We start with a look at a challenging support client, discuss the different kinds of support you can provide, outline the key topics for an effective support orientation, and argue the importance of being responsive. We also provide tips you can use to deal with a common problem faced by project managers: supporting a project your team did not build. We conclude by outlining an easy technique you can use to provide effective proactive support.

Support and Operations

Sam the Entrepreneur

Sam is an entrepreneur who runs a small business that sells a variety of specialty computer components from a busy web site. He has two staff members who help run the business out of Sam's garage, handling fulfillment. Sam's business has very tight margins, and he is accustomed to running a no-frills operation.

For years, Sam has run his web site using individual consultants who help handle development and support. The consultants all have regular jobs and support Sam's company on the side to earn extra money. As Sam's web site has grown in complexity, he finds that the part-time consultants are not able to keep up with his demands—and importantly—provide support when he demands it.

A few months ago, Sam hired an offshore firm that promised to have two developers working full-time on his web site for only a little more than he was paying his last consultant. This worked out well for a month, until Sam noticed that various parts of his web site stopped working and he had trouble communicating clearly with the developers on the project.

Finally, Sam decided to hire a local web consulting firm to manage his web site. He was surprised at how much more the firm charged than his previous consultants. He decided that it might be worth it if the firm could solve some of his recurring problems and implement several new features that had been stalled for months.

Sam was dismayed when the firm required an initial audit of the web site. The audit was expensive and turned up more than 20 security and performance problems. Sam initially thought that the consulting firm was trying to take advantage of him and sent the audit to his previous consultant, who validated the majority of the issues and reminded Sam that he had also warned him about these problems.

Sam agreed to implement the most critical security fixes, but refused to address some of the others. He wanted the new firm to focus on a few stalled projects. The new relationship worked out well, and Sam was very happy with the new consulting firm—especially the project manager—who provided regular progress reports and communicated clearly.

Sam increasingly relied on the new firm—including calling for emergency after-hours support—whenever he had an issue that needed to be resolved. After all, what else is emergency support for?

As project costs continued to increase, Sam felt that he had become an important client. Sam used a technique that had been successful for him with other service providers. He became more demanding and began refusing to pay certain costs for which he did not think he should be responsible. After all, he was in business to make money—not pay a consulting firm. And since he needed to keep his margins thin, so did the consulting firm.

Sometimes the company would run into problems with the low-cost software or approach Sam requested the firm use to save money. Sam would hold firm on these cost overruns. After a particularly egregious problem—where a new module that the firm was building conflicted with a component of the server that Sam had earlier refused to upgrade—Sam pushed back and refused to pay for the work. "I'm keeping these guys in line," he thought.

Sam was startled and angry to receive a letter from his consulting firm advising him that they would be discontinuing services within 60 days. "I can't believe that these jerks don't want my business," Sam thinks.

The primary challenge with Sam the Entrepreneur was that the true cost of support was not made clear. When the security-and-performance audit was presented to Sam, it was clear that he was not ready to invest in the level of support that the firm needed to provide. This mismatched expectation foreshadowed the issues to come, and it may have been better for the two parties not to have made a support agreement in the first place.

The transition from completed project to support is a delicate one that requires careful management of expectations. In addition to outlining how to make the transition into support, in this chapter we also look in detail at how to effectively provide support on projects you did not develop. We also discuss the importance of support orientations and providing quick responses to your clients. Finally, we wrap up with a simple technique you can use to provide proactive support to your client.

Providing Support

Hopefully, your projects will launch successfully, be used and leveraged by the client, and thrive for years. No matter how well-designed and documented and implemented and tested, however, an application in active use will always need periodic enhancements. This is natural. Businesses change, workflows change, personnel changes. Your client may want to move more workflows than were originally intended onto your platform once it proves stable and easy to use.

After managing a project from development through launch, you will often be asked to take the lead on providing ongoing support. There are really two ways support work can be arranged:

- **Ad hoc**. In this model, the client e-mails you asking for a modification and they are billed for the time it takes to make the refinement. There is no task queue, regular patch schedule, or predictable rate of requests. A better name for this kind of support might be "Inbox triage."
- **Monthly support**. With regular support, your client has access to a set amount of time (often a set number of hours per month, or one large retainer) from which to draw when working on refinements. For anything beyond 4 hours a month or 16 hours in a single retainer, you likely will have a laundry list of refinements to work on.

Generally, the most important component to providing great support is to *enjoy the process* of providing great customer service. The phrase "customer service" has become a loaded statement because some companies think that hanging a sign with "provide great customer service" on the office wall will actually make their employees care.

As any trip to a dilapidated rental car office will tell you, this is **decidedly not true**. What does help is if you enjoy taking care of clients and take pride in your work. If you get a little smile in your mind when you think about the last time you made a client happy, then you do not need this tip. If you find that you do not enjoy working with clients, being a project manager may be exceptionally challenging.

Beyond learning to enjoy taking care of your customers, here are some specific tips for providing great ad hoc support:

- **Be responsive** (see "Be Responsive," later in this chapter).
- **Fix everything two ways**. Software blogger Joel Spolsky coined this phrase in his excellent article, "Seven Steps to Remarkable Customer Service" (see the reading list provided in the Appendix). Fixing everything two ways is pretty simple: Fix the issue that happened (immediate) and fix what caused the issue to happen in the first place (deeper issue). When you get an ad hoc support request, take a moment to think, "What else can we do to prevent this or something similar from happening again?" Ask the developer this question if you are stuck. Fixing it completely when the first issue report comes in might take longer than just addressing the immediate issue, but it will take less time than dealing with it when it happens again (and it will).
- **Be honest**. If this issue was something you or the team did wrong, admit as much clearly and succinctly. Then move on.

Long-term Support

In a long-term support environment, you likely have a list of feature requests and issues provided by the client for the project. You likely will also have some sense from the client and your own knowledge of the project on which tasks are a priority.

One of the best ways to improve monthly/retainer support is through patch management. Instead of completing and pushing each refinement individually to production, bundle several refinements into a single patch that is installed as a unit to the production server. You can push individual completed features to a staging server (see tips later in this section) as you complete tasks for the forthcoming patch.

This has several benefits:

- You will move the client away from always wanting *just one more change pushed this afternoon.* That kind of hectic patch schedule is stressful to your developers, inefficient, and inaccurate.
- You will save the client time by having to perform the patch process once for several features, rather than once per feature.
- You can maintain momentum and force client decisions by using a patch schedule. Pick a set date—say, the third Monday of every month—to automatically kick off bundling of all completed tasks in the past month into a patch for review and deployment.

We have used this **patch schedule** successfully with many clients:

1. On the third Monday of the month, bundle up all completed tasks into a patch.

2. Deploy the patch to the staging server.

3. Send a patch summary e-mail to the client with a list of the completed items in the patch and links to the staging server for their review. State that you will need final feedback by Tuesday at close of business and that the patch will be installed live on Thursday.

4. On Thursday, deploy the patch.

5. Send a summary e-mail to the client that the patch was successful.

6. The following week, prepare a summary e-mail to the client outlining what is to be included in the next patch and what items remain in the hold queue. (See the following additional tips.)

Here are some additional tips for providing outstanding monthly/retainer support:

- **Use a staging server**. You should always deploy a refinement to a staging server first for proper testing and client review. A staging server is a system set up as similar to production as possible (hardware, location, network connection, real and recent data, installed components, configuration, etc.) and that has access limited to just your team and the client's team.
- **Keep your patches small**. Even with a month between patches, you will only have time for four or five refinements. Just accept that higher priority items will appear from the client without warning and that tasks will take longer than anticipated. Keep your initial patch list small.

- **Develop a checklist** for deploying patches to production to ensure that a consistent, high-quality deployment process is maintained over time.
- **Send a summary e-mail** when you start working on a new patch. Prepare an e-mail to the client that clearly lists the four or five items you have put into the next patch and all of the remaining items in the hold queue when you start a patch. State that you will proceed with these items unless you hear otherwise. This gives your client a chance to alter priorities, but also ensures that you have a decision preloaded into the interaction to move forward. Momentum and onward!
- **Be proactive**. With a limited set of support, your client may often be reluctant to make decisions because those decisions have a measurable impact on how much support time they have left. Help them make decisions by using proactive project management (see "Proactive Project Management" in Chapter 6 for more information).
- **Leave a little extra time**. If you have a monthly retainer it will be helpful to leave a small chunk of time unused to deal with unexpected support issues that tend to arise.

Support Orientation

Regardless of the type of support you will provide, consider holding a brief support orientation call with your client. This call can serve many purposes:

- It makes explicit the level of support you will be providing;
- It clearly marks the shift from development to support; and
- It makes sure your client knows how to request support.

Consider preparing a brief outline of the major topics you want to discuss. These might include

- How to request support (e-mail, telephone, ticketing system, etc.)
- Expected response time
- Financial details of the support plan (for example, if there is a maintenance plan or if it is hourly)
- What support does (and does not) include
- What to do in an emergency if the site goes down

Urban Insight (see Figure 11-1) has achieved a 90% 5-year client retention rate. We have found that support orientations can dramatically improve your long-term ability to support your clients by making sure that clients understand what to expect.

Client Name
Drupal Support Subscription Orientation

Purpose
- Introduce you to how Urban Insight provides ongoing support for your website.

How to Request Support
- Email us (Preferred): support@urbaninsight.com
- Call us: 877-872-6150
- Fax us: 877-944-6792

What Happens Next?
- Request goes into our Case tracking system.
- Within 4-8 hours, a team member evaluates the request.
- If request can be resolved in less than 2 hours, we perform the work.
- Within 2 business days, request is completed.
- If more information is required, or the request requires more than 2 hours, we contact you with an estimate and timeline for completion.
- Case number and description appears on your monthly invoice.

How to Report a Problem
- What were you trying to do?
- What did you expect to happen?
- What actually happened?
- What browser, browser version, and operating system are you using? (For example: Firefox 4 on Mac OSX 10.6 or Internet Explorer 9 on Windows 7)

Introducing Your Support Team
- First level support: Ron, Van, Cate
- Second level support: Minnur, Ki

Authorized Callers
- Who is authorized to call on your behalf?
- Up to 2 contacts
- We need for each: Name, email, telephone
- We need one security passphrase for your organization (ie: "The dog is in Kansas")

Drupal Update Subscription
- Security patches, other updates released approximately monthly.
- We schedule updates to be performed Monday through Thursday at an agreed-upon time between 9am and 4pm PT (to ensure maximum availability of Urban Insight and client staff for 24 hours in the unlikely need of maximum support).
- We notify you when we will perform the update.
- We estimate 2 hours to perform the updates, although typical website offline time is about 15 minutes.
- We perform the update and perform QA testing.
- We notify you when the update is complete.

Figure 11-1. A support orientation template (detail; shows first of two pages)

Be Responsive

Over all of the projects, challenges, successes, failures, mistakes, oversights, miscommunications, and badly handled expectations, there is one central trick that will help maintain a positive relationship with the client time and time again: **be responsive**.

If you take one thing from this entire book, it should be this: being available and responsive always generates appreciation from the client and sets your interactions with them apart from the others with whom they deal.

Remember, to the client you are just a vendor, like a plumber or an electrician. You have promised to do some task that they do not know how to do themselves and for which you charge a lot of money. Anyone would feel powerless in this relationship. Being responsive and available will make the client feel more in control of the situation and more confident in the outcome.

Why?

Because when things go badly, being responsive makes it easy for the client to handle internal questions about the problem. Say the client e-mails you about an issue and you reply within half an hour that you are aware of the issue and you have someone looking into it. Your client can happily answer a call from his or her boss and say, "Yes, I've let the consultants know about it and they said they are looking into it right now." That is a much better answer than, "I let them know but I haven't heard back."

Uncertainty breeds doubt, confusion, and anger. Constant updates, responsiveness, and easy access alleviate most concerns. Since checking your e-mail can reduce your productivity, consider spending 10 or so minutes each hour checking your e-mail so you can quickly respond to clients, put out fires, and nudge developers in the right direction.

Supporting Projects Developed by Someone Else

It is challenging to provide ongoing support (issue fixes, new features, training, etc.) on a project that your team did not develop. The project is unfamiliar, it was not developed to your standards, and you might be blamed later on for poor decisions made by the initial developers.

Here are the top five challenges in providing client support, complete with tips to help mitigate them:

Challenge #1: The Project Is a Mess

The greatest challenge to taking on support for any project is the quality of the project itself. The fact that the original developers were not selected to provide support probably indicates that the relationship with the client was not positive. If the relationship was not handled well, the development of the software probably was not either.

Challenge #2: The Client Has Unrealistic Expectations About the Schedule

By the time you take over support, the client has likely been building a large wish list of feature requests and issues, all of which appear to be urgent to the client.

Challenge #3: The Development Workflow is Not Set Up Correctly

To support a project properly, you need a production system and a staging system, which lives in the same place as the production system and uses similar hardware and software. This often does not exist in projects you take over.

Challenge #4: The Site Lacks Stability

The site is generally unstable and critical issues occur at least once a month with no decrease in frequency. These could be problems with the hardware, the network, the software itself, the design of the interface, or a combination of these factors.

Challenge #5: The Client is Not Well Informed

If the client is coming to you for support, then the relationship with the original developers has probably soured. If this is the case, then it is likely that the client has not had assistance with the site for some time, and when they did, they did not feel informed or updated of progress.

Pointer #1: Start Support with a Project Review and Recommendations Document

A great way to protect your team against starting support on a problematic project is to perform a review of the application and prepare a summary recommendations document. The summary recommendations document is a listing of all of the problems with the project, complete with a short description of what to do to address each issue. You can organize the recommendations into three sections: high priority, medium priority, and low priority.

When you deliver the document to the client, clearly state that you will begin working down this list of recommendations in tandem with whatever new features and issue refinements the client has requested.

A recommendations document has many advantages:

- It provides your team time to get acquainted with the application.
- The review should identify all of the problems in the site so you are not surprised later.
- You can clearly state all of the site's problems ahead of time should a more serious problem develop later.
- The review offers the opportunity to make additional recommendations to further bring the project to your own standards.

Pointer #2: Don't Overtly Blame the Previous Development Team

Focus on addressing the issue with the client's best interests in mind. If the client asks, you can state that this was a mistake of the previous developers. But you do not want to get in the habit of blaming the previous team for two important reasons:

- The client selected the previous team. Reminders of any mistakes of this team may be taken personally by the client.

- Placing blame is unseemly and reduces your credibility. Take responsibility and move forward.

Pointer #3: Use Regular Patches to Maintain Momentum, but Save Time on Deployment

Patches let you queue up several refinements together so that you can release them to production as a group, which is more efficient than releasing them one at a time. If you start using the patch language with the client you can schedule regular releases (read: monthly), which has the effect of maintaining momentum with development and keeping the client focused by having a release date to share with colleagues.

Pointer #4: Take the Time to Set Up the Right Workflow

At the start of the project, take the extra time to set up the proper development workflow. This likely includes

- A password-protected staging server
- A way to easily sync the data from production to staging
- Bringing the code under version control
- Bringing the staging and production sites under version control
- Bringing the database under version control

Pointer #5: Provide Regular Updates

Communication is vital and builds confidence between you and your client. Take the time to write a detailed but clear[1] summary of all outstanding tasks, regardless of whether they are in development, on hold, queued for the next release, or complete.

---

[1] Clarity first, concise often.

Bonus Pointer: Use a Monthly Checklist to Proactively Identify Issues

A great way to increase the stability of a project is to put together a checklist that you can run each month on the system to look for common indicators that will cause more serious problems throughout the entire stack of the project. See "The Launch Checklist" in Chapter 10 for more information.

Pretend You're Leaving

Justin occasionally spends a few moments thinking to himself, "If I was leaving tomorrow and showing my replacement everything they had to know to take over, what would I be embarrassed about handing over? What project or site or module just isn't where it should be?"

It's likely that something—some project, module, web site, section, or configuration—is going to come to mind, something that was not finished right, was not completed to your own standards or those of your organization, or something that is just so slapdash that you need to finish it *the right way*.

This situation commonly happens when a project is in support, and not in active development. While developing a project is a proactive task—you lead the team that is seeking out what needs to be built and are building it—support is often a reactive process, in that you and your team act only when there is something that needs to be fixed or the client asks for something new.

In such a reactive environment, it's easy for non-critical tasks to be consistently deprioritized over incoming support requests. But this sort of "cruft" does build up over time and could eventually impact your project. If possible, it's best to address these items as quickly as you reasonably can, to prevent any pile from forming.

Whatever does come to mind, fix it. This little embarrassment gnawing at the back of your head is the most likely topic to come up without warning in a meeting (thus requiring embarrassing answers) or to have some kind of system issue that interrupts the client's ability to do work.

You do not need to do this often, but when you do, it is revealing.

Wrapping Up

We've come to the end of the road, both for our book and our sample project. It is our hope that the hard-earned lessons in this book will increase your effectiveness as a project manager, and save you a little pain in the process. We've shown you how to move a project from an idea into a signed scope of work, from a set of requirements to a working beta, and from a launched project to post-project support.

Not every project will neatly follow this process. Many projects will not use every step we outlined, or you may only be involved in specific stages. We also tried to provide specific advice on common tasks in the life of a web project manager, including writing professional e-mails, creating checklists to ensure consistent quality, running effective meetings, and extracting what is needed from your client to ensure a successful project.

We've covered the mundane but critical tasks, such as how to write an agenda, how to gather requirements, how to prepare a project schedule, and how to take notes. We've talked about difficult situations, like handling out-of-scope requests, getting answers from reluctant clients, and keeping an eye on your team without micromanaging.

In some ways, the job of the project manager is unglamorous. You schedule meetings, you take notes, you keep the project moving, and you watch the project budget like a cheap father obsessing over the thermostat.

A great day for a project manager ends with sending a clear summary from an effective meeting and a quick glance at an on-schedule project budget. It is the developers and the designers and the wireframers and the technical architects who get to exercise their creativity. It is you, the project manager, who "herds cats" and makes the project successful.

Without effective project management, designers and developers and architects would have far fewer projects to work on, far fewer interesting problems to solve, and far fewer opportunities for creation.

Project management is sometimes a bit like roadwork. As long as you keep the potholes filled and traffic moving, your team takes your work for granted. But as soon as someone hits a pothole, well...

However, those clients who have experienced poor project management (and many have) will quickly recognize your project management acumen, and you will become a sought-after team member because people will remember your calm efficiency and competence.

If it was possible to have a project free of problems, there would be no need for project management. While we believe that the advice in this book will serve you well in your future endeavors, we know that your challenges will be unique and varied. We would like to leave you with some parting advice that we hope will be helpful in your professional life, be it project management or otherwise.

Be unflappable, positive, and persistent.

Appendix

Project Management Software

New products are coming out all the time to help with project communication, collaboration, and general management. At the time of this writing, here are several notable tools that we use and like:

- **FogBugz** (Fog Creek Software): A web-based project management tool featuring robust support for issue tracking, scheduling, and estimating accuracy history. About $25 per person per month. *Very powerful, if a bit complex.*

- **ZenDesk.com** – A web-based issue-tracking tool. Around $29 per month per user.

- **Basecamp** (37signals): An elegantly designed, web-based team collaboration tool focused on ease of use and simplicity. Robust support for team communication, milestone scheduling, and to-do items. About $100 per month for ateam. *Your clients who like to use the web will love this tool.*

- **Balsamiq Mockups** (Balsamiq Studios): An easy-to-use wireframing software. $79 per user, one-time. *Makes wire framing fun again.*

- **Visio** (Microsoft): A tool for creating diagrams and flow charts, which you can use for wire frames. About $100 per user.

- **MockFlow**: A web-based (with offline support) collaborative wireframing tool. $79 per year for a team.

- **OmniGraffle**: A Mac-only desktop tool for diagraming. $99 per user.

- **UserTesting.com**: An online tool to outsource usability testing to the crowd. $39 per test.
- **Google Docs (Google)**: For sharing and collaboratively editing documents, checklists, and project management documents informally (and sometimes formally), Google Docs has emerged as a favorite. Free.

Reading List

There is a lot of great writing that expands on the topics in this book. We recommend the following:

- **"Alertbox,"** by Jakob Neilson
  www.useit.com/alertbox/
- **"Seven Steps to Remarkable Customer Service,"** by Joel Spolsky
  www.joelonsoftware.com/articles/customerservice.html
- **"Painless Functional Specifications,"** parts 1, 2, 3, and 4, by Joel Spolsky
  www.joelonsoftware.com/articles/fog0000000036.html
- **"The Iceberg Secret, Revealed,"** by Joel Spolsky
  www.joelonsoftware.com/articles/fog0000000356.html
- **"Usability Testing with Morae,"** by Joel Spolsky
  www.joelonsoftware.com/articles/UsabilityTestingwithMorae.html
- **"The Project Aardvark Spec,"** by Joel Spolsky
  www.joelonsoftware.com/articles/AardvarkSpec.html
- **"Usability 101: Introduction to Usability,"** by Jakob Nielsen
  www.useit.com/alertbox/20030825.html
- **"The Checklist,"** by Atul Gawande, *The New Yorker*
  www.newyorker.com/reporting/2007/12/10/071210fa_fact_gawande
- ***Getting Things Done***, by David Allen
  https://secure.davidco.com/store/catalog/GETTING-THINGS-DONE-PAPERBACK-p-16175.php
- **"The Mythical Man Month: Essays on Software Engineering,"** by Fred Brooks

Document Templates

Here you will find a series of document templates for the different kinds of client-facing documents we discussed in the book. We tried to make them descriptive enough to be instructive but generic enough to be usable.

Web Site Kick-Off Meeting Agenda

Client Name

PROJECT NAME

9:00 am–11:00 am PT
Monday, January 24, 2013
Address, City, State, ZIP

AGENDA

- Meeting Purpose: Understand the project requirements

  1. Introductions (5 min)

  2. Confirm Project Scope (5 min)

  3. Review Process (5 min)

  4. Discuss Project Requirements (60 min)

- General Information
- Web Site Purpose
- Features
- Creative Brief
- Information Architecture Brief
- Technical Brief

  5. Create Initial Wireframes (30 min)

  6. Next Steps, Wrap-up (5 min)

Participants:

- Name, Affiliation

Web Site Requirements Document

Client Name

PROJECT NAME

Prepared for:	Client Name (client@email.com) Another Client Name (client@email.edu)
Prepared by:	Your Name (you@name.com) Another Author (another@name.com)
Prepared on:	January 1, 2013
Version:	1.0 / January 1, 2013
File name:	02-web-requirements-document.docx

Document Approvals:

_____

Client Name   Date
Client Organization

_____

Author Name   Date
Author Organization

ge Control	Author	Version	Change Reference
ary 1, 2013	Author Name	0.1	No previous document. Created initial draft ba on current understanding of project as templat kick-off meeting.

Section 1: Purpose of Web Site

Official Web Site Name What is the official name of the web site?	
Objectives What are the business and marketing objectives of the project (for example, to increase membership, promote content, increase sales)?	
Target Audiences & Characteristics Who are the primary audiences? Identify a few unique characteristics about each audience.	
Key Target Actions What is the primary action (or actions) you want the user to take from the main page of your web site? (Examples: Sign up, purchase, download, move along a specific path, call.)	
Key Target Audience Insight What is the most compelling thing you want the target audience to think after they experience the web site?	

Subject **Question or issue summary.**	Add additional questions necessary to define your project.

Section 2: Features

[Note: Specific features and functionality identified in the scope or contract should be listed here.]

Web Pages How many unique pages will be developed for the site? For how many of those will the content be transferred from a legacy web site?	
Data What specific database content will be imported into the system (accounts, data, articles, transactions, etc.)?	
Navigation How will the navigation be presented (horizontal, vertical, dropdown, etc.)?	
Breadcrumbs Will the navigation system include breadcrumbs?	

Event List and Calendar Which format will be used for identifying event dates, a grid calendar or event list? How frequently will events occur?	
Newsletters How will users sign up on the web site? What data will we collect for subscribers? How many lists will be created?	
Web Site Search What search service or engine will be used?	
Contact Form Fields What fields should be collected on the contact form?	▪ Name ▪ E-mail address
Images What is the source for images?	
Web Analytics What Web analytics system will be used?	

Subject **Question or issue summary.**	Add additional questions necessary to define your project.

Section 3: Creative Brief

Creative Deliverable What will be delivered based on this brief?	<ul><li>Three home page designs</li><li>Two rounds of home page design</li><li>Three typical content page designs</li><li>One round of content page design</li></ul>
Tagline Do you have a tagline that should appear on the web site?	<ul><li></li></ul>
Design Comparison Identify 3–5 designs that you like and discuss what you like about them.	1. 2. 3. 4. 5.

Competitive Landscape Identify by name and URL the web sites of three competitors, and identify what you like or dislike about their web sites.	1. 2. 3.
Browser Orientation What is the expected browser size? Will the design be fluid or fixed width?	■ ■
Design Feel Describe the overall feeling or perception the web site should convey. (Examples: conservative, green, progressive, friendly, formal, casual, professional, energetic.)	
Required Branding What are the branding elements that should appear on every page? (Examples: organization name, tagline, logo.)	■ ■ ■
Logo / Identity Design Do you have an identity stylesheet, guidelines, or requirements? If so, please attach a copy to this brief.	

Colors What colors do you prefer? What colors should not be used?	Preferred Colors ▪ Colors not to be used ▪
Fonts Do you have preferred or required fonts?	
Images Identify by name three images that should/could appear on the home page.	1. 2. 3.
Assets to Be Provided What assets will be provided to create the web site design? (Examples: logo image file, photo images, sample text.) Who will provide these assets?	▪ Logo ▪
Subject **Question or issue summary.**	▪ Add additional questions necessary to define your project.

Section 4: Information Architecture Brief

Home Page Elements What are the additional branding or content elements that should appear on the home page?	- Logo - Tagline - Organization title - Primary navigation - Rotating image set - News items - Featured news item - Event listing
Content Page Header Elements	- Search - E-mail Signup - Login/Registration (Logout/My Account)
Navigation Categories What are the top-level navigation categories that will appear on every page?	-
Sub-Navigation Will the site require sub-navigation menus?	-
Footer What should appear on page footers?	© 2013 Organization Name Terms of Service I Privacy Policy I Contact Us I Accessibility

Tagging How will content be tagged?	
Information Categories (Tax-onomies) Identify terms that represent standard groupings of informa-tion that would be useful to site visitors and organization staff.	▪
Types of Content Identify the unique types of con-tent that will be created on the web site. (Examples: news, events, articles, biographies.)	▪
Internationalization What languages will the web site support? Will all pages be translated into all languages? Who will provide translations?	▪
Subject *Question or issue summary.*	▪ Add additional questions necessary to define your project.

Section 5: Technical Brief

Content Management System What content management system will be used?	
Technical Requirements What technology platform will be used?	▪
Internal Users How many web site authors will be updating the web site?	
Roles What are the various administrative functions, and what level of authority will each function need?	▪ Administrator
Workflow Process What will the process be for developing content, submitting content, and approving content before it is published?	▪

Public User Accounts with Login Will public or registered members need to log in to the web site to comment on articles or participate in discussion forums?	▪
Section 508 Will the web site comply with Section 508 accessibility requirements?	
Domain Names What are the domain names involved in this project?	
Domain Registrar Who is your domain registrar? Who controls access to your registry account?	
Website Hosting Who will be providing web site hosting? Who will provide development and staging servers?	▪
Support Program Who will be providing ongoing support?	▪

Security Considerations Describe any special security precautions warranted.	
Subject *Question or issue summary.*	▪ Add additional questions necessary to define your project.

Section 6: Search Engine Optimization Brief

Website Description for Search Engines In 150 characters, describe the purpose of your web site as you would like it to appear in search engine results listing.	
Twitter What is your Twitter account? How will we integrate with Twitter?	▪
Facebook What is your Facebook page/account/app? How will we integrate with Facebook?	▪ ▪

Yelp, LinkedIn, etc. What other social media accounts should we know about?	▪
Legacy Analytics/Web Master Accounts? Are there existing analytics or web master accounts that we should preserve?	▪
Keywords and Phrases What are the top keywords and phrases you wish to appear in search engines?	▪
Market Areas What are the primary market areas in which you wish to be recognized?	▪
Page Titles Should we auto-set page titles on content creation?	▪
Automatic URLs Should we auto-set URLs on content creation?	▪
Inbound Links Identify a few sites and contacts that are likely to link to your new web site.	▪

Directories/References Identify a few industry-specific directories or sites that are likely to include a link to your web site.	▪
Domain Name Standardization Multiple forms of domains names are penalized. Do you prefer www.domain.com or domain.com, or some other variant?	▪
Subject *Question or issue summary.*	▪ Add additional questions necessary to define your project.

Section 7: Other Considerations

Organizational Decision-Making Team Who will the decision-making team include? What decisions will require executive or board sign-off? How must the decision-making process be factored into the project schedule?	▪
Subject Question or issue summary.	▪ Add additional questions necessary to define your project.

Technical Requirements Document

Client Name

PROJECT NAME

Prepared for:	Client Name (client@email.com) Another Client Name (client@email.edu)
Prepared by:	Your Name (you@name.com) Another Author (another@name.com)
Prepared on:	January 1, 2013
Version:	1.0 / January 1, 2013
Filename:	03-tech-requirements-document.doc

Document Approvals:

_____   Date
Client Name
Client Organization

_____   Date
Author Name
Author Organization

Change Control	Author	Version	Change Reference
January 1, 2013	Author Name	0.1	No previous document. Created initial draft based on current understanding of project as template for kick-off meeting.

1. Project Overview and Goals

If this project has high-level goals that the client would appreciate seeing called out, list them here. Otherwise, remove this section.

2. Functional Requirements—Core System

A short introduction can be included, but only if necessary.

Reqmt ID	Description	Custom Dev
R1.1	*List every feature.*	n/a
R1.2	*Each line should call out a specific requirement.*	n/a
R1.3	*For ease of review and reference, group the requirements by project component.*	n/a
R1.4	EXAMPLE: System interface will run inside of a web browser (Microsoft Internet Explorer version 8 or above or Mozilla Firefox version 3 or above).	n/a
R1.5	EXAMPLE: System will use latest stable release of Drupal.	n/a
R1.6	EXAMPLE: System will include up to five content types, including story (for all articles/posts), wiki, blog (for individual user blogs), and page (for static content).	n/a
R1.7	EXAMPLE: System will automatically generate friendly URLs.	n/a

4. Function Requirements—Home and Story

Reqmt ID	Description	Custom Dev
R1.8	*This is another section. Underline changes after the first version for ease of review.*	n/a
R1.9	EXAMPLE: Story node will include a custom field for identifying one or more authors of a story.	✓ Medium

4. Function Requirements—Rich Media

Reqmt ID	Description	Custom Dev
R1.10	EXAMPLE: System will include a rich text editor, for using complex formatting in the creation of body text.	n/a

4. Function Requirements—Editor Control Panel

Reqmt ID	Description	Custom Dev
R1.11	EXAMPLE: System will include a rich text editor for using complex formatting in the creation of body text.	n/a
R1.12	EXAMPLE: Editor Control Panel (ECP) will store presentation information in custom fields on story nodes.	✓ High
R1.13		

6. Function Requirements—Mobile Integration

Reqm t ID	Description
R1.14	*The "Custom Dev" column is not always necessary. The column was added to this project to call out to the client features that would require custom development effort to achieve. This was used to help manage expectations about scope.*
R1.15	EXAMPLE: System will allow users to contribute content via MMS.

7. Function Requirements—E-mail Newsletters

Reqmt ID	Description
R1.16	EXAMPLE: System will support plain text and HTML e-mail newsletters.
R1.17	EXAMPLE: System will allow users to create reusable templates for composing and sending e-mail newsletters.

8. Function Requirements—SEO Optimization

Reqmt ID	Description
R1.18	EXAMPLE: System will integrate with Google Webmaster tools.
R1.19	EXAMPLE: System will include automatic Google sitemap integration.

9. Function Requirements—Permissions and Roles

Reqmt ID	Description
R1.20	*Understanding how system permissions should be set up is vital to building client creditability. Mistakes in system permissions can lead to frustrating client surprises.*

R1.21	EXAMPLE: System will include roles for student contributors, student editors, and site administrators.

10. Function Requirements—Content Migration

Reqm t ID	Description
R1.22	*Migrations can be very complex. It's wise to put clear boundaries here to manage complexity creep in the import task during development and launch.*
R1.23	EXAMPLE: System will migrate existing site user accounts (but not pass-words).
R1.24	EXAMPLE: Content migration will include up to 250 stories, 100 videos, and 100 audio files.

11. Technology Requirements

[Your Firm] assumes that the server hardware and all software licenses will be provided by [Client Name], and the [Client] IT staff will install and configure all necessary software required for application functionality.

Reqm t ID	Description
R1.25	*Assumptions are dangerous. Spell everything out.*
R1.26	EXAMPLE: System will run on server class hardware.
R1.27	EXAMPLE: System will be built using the LAMP platform: Linux, Apache, MySQL, and PHP.

3. Security Requirements (Recommendations)

The following requirements are recommendations for the [Client] IT staff based on our shared goal of providing a highly secure application.

Reqm t ID	Description
R1.28	*This is an important section to clearly spell out expectations for security. While you can't force these on the client, it's important to be on the record about these items should a security breach occur later. **The authors take security very seriously**.*
R1.29	EXAMPLE: A minimum number of local machine accounts will be established, and only for system administration purposes.
R1.30	EXAMPLE: A hardware firewall will restrict access to the system by IP and port.
R1.31	EXAMPLE: A software firewall will restrict access to the system by IP and port.
R1.32	EXAMPLE: Default firewall policies will be to deny all access, enabling only specific access as needed.
R1.33	EXAMPLE: Remote access (via SSH) will be restricted by IP address to specific hosts, and will connect via a non-standard port.
R1.34	EXAMPLE: Physical server hardware will be located in a secured location.
R1.35	EXAMPLE: Operating system security logging will be enabled.
R1.36	EXAMPLE: [Client] IT staff will review server security log and application log at least monthly, and preferably weekly.
R1.37	EXAMPLE: [Client] IT staff will regularly apply all security patches for major systems components (OS, Apache, MySQL, PHP, SSH).
R1.38	EXAMPLE: [Your Firm] will develop a weekly security and system health evaluation checklist to proactively monitor the system.

4. Project Risks

Sometimes it's helpful to clearly call out the risks of the project.

Any technology development project entails certain risks. During the requirements gathering process, [Your Firm] asked various stakeholders about what risks they could foresee in rolling out Drupal as a core technology component for support of academic programs. This risk analysis section is a summary of those findings.

Scope creep can best be mitigated by conducting robust requirements gathering and creating a specific, thorough, and detailed outline of all project requirements prior to development. While additional modifications identified after development has started can be worked into the project, they are best left to a follow-up phase after launch.

In addition, [Your Firm] suggests using the Basecamp project management tool, which helps streamline communication from stakeholders, track key schedule milestones, and assign action items and follow-ups to stakeholders.

5. Appendix

Any items for reference can be included here.

Web Site Technical Specification

Client Name

PROJECT NAME

Prepared for:	Client Name (client@email.com) Another Client Name (client@email.edu)
Prepared by:	Your Name (you@name.com) Another Author (another@name.com)
Prepared on:	January 1, 2013
Version:	1.0 / January 1, 2013
Filename:	04-tech-spec.docx

Document Approvals:

_____

Client Name   Date
Client Organization

_____

Author Name   Date
Author Organization

Change Control	Author	Version	Change Reference
January 1, 2013	Author Name	0.1	No previous document. Created initial draft based on current understanding of project as template for kick-off meeting.

Overview

The editorial control panel (ECP) tool allows users to manage the content of the site. Using the ECP tool site editors create home pages to expose as the site home page or as section home pages.

There are three key concepts of the ECP system:

1. **Templates** are built-in, pre-designed layouts that define the arrangement of visual elements on the page, but do not offer specifics, such as individual story placement.

2. **Storyboards** define the specific story position and selection for a specific template. The system tracks an unlimited number of storyboards and each storyboard is based on one template.

3. Storyboards are made up of customizable **box types** that allow the user to customize content. The placement and arrangement of these boxes is saved to the template, but the specific content and customization of the boxes are tied to storyboards.

The ECP is a custom module in Drupal. Using this module editors, you can:

- Create new storyboards
- Edit existing storyboards
- Delete storyboards
- Set the active site home page storyboard
- Set the active section home page storyboards
- Define the time frame for the most ready stories and most commented stories box

The ECP is agnostic to section home pages and the site home page; the editor simply always has one storyboard assigned to the site home page and one to each section home page. For a **preview function** in the system, we can simply create a section called "preview" that isn't linked to the public site, and editors can set the storyboard they are working on to that section for reviewing.

The basic workflow of **editorial actions** on the site is:

1. Editor creates a new storyboard.
2. Editor refines new storyboard, adjusting story layout, selection, etc.

3.　Editor saves the storyboard while working.

4.　Editor then closes the storyboard and chooses which story board is on the home page and which is on the section home pages.

Homepage Templates and Box Types

The homepage templates[1] are:

- Template 1: Typical Day—Lead story, two features
- Template 2: Breaking News—One lead story package
- Template 3: Slow Day— Carousel and Promo Box
- Template 4: Section Front Page[2]
- Template 5: Breaking News— One lead story package with large image
    - This template is the same as the "T2: Breaking News" template, with the difference that the top story box allows for wide image.
    - The wide image box uses "Custom text lead story box" box type.

In addition to these five templates, there is a special template used for all blog home pages.

Each of these templates is composed of a unique arrangement of 14 standard box types. Each box is edited in the ECP by the same method, but templates have varying numbers of each box type and not all of them are used on each template.

When working on a storyboard, the editor will really be working on each of the specific standard box types that make up the template used in the storyboard.

1.　Box Type 1: Single lead story (M)

a.　Used on T1 and T4

---

[1] See wire frames version 4.

[2] Although called section front page, this template, like all other home page templates, is available for section home pages or the site home page.

    b.   Editor selects a single story; ECP automatically sets the title, author, teaser, related links

    c.   Editor selects which piece of rich media will appear: image, video, slide show, MP3

2.   Box Type 2: Large single lead story (M)

    a.   Used on T2

    b.   Same as "Single lead story" but this box is wider and the media piece is larger

3.   Box Type 3: Lead story gallery (H)

    a.   Used on T3

    b.   Editor selects one or more stories; ECP automatically sets title, author, teaser, and image thumbnail

    c.   OPEN ISSUE: What do we do if the story has no image?

    d.   Gallery controls only appear if two or more stories selected

4. Box Type 4: Single story mini box (M)

    a.   Used on TI, T2, T3, T4, and T%

    b.   Editor selects story; ECP automatically sets title, author, teaser and thumbnail

    c.   OPEN ISSUE: What do we do if the story has no image?

    d.   Editor sets box display title; if blank, this is filled in with name of story section

5.   Box Type 5: Wide single story mini box (M)

    a.   Used on TI, T2, T3, and T5

    b.   Same as "Single story mini box" but wider, with different image placement

    c.   Includes "Showcase links" automatically displayed under story

       i. Selected by matching stories of boxes story category

      ii. Sort by Story.Rank, Story.Published, Story.Title

     iii. Show three stories

     iv. Only show these stories when the storyboard is active and being used; during editing; just include a box that says "Showcases links will appear here"

   d. Includes an editor-selectable toggle to "Show blogs drop-down"

       i. When checked, box will show a drop-down menu that includes the name of each blog hosted on site

      ii. The blog drop-down will take the user to that blog when selected

6.   Box Type 6: Wide two-story mini box (L)

   a.   Used on T1

   b.   Same as "Wide single story mini box," but includes two stories instead of one and does not include Showcase links

7.   Box Type 7: Multimedia player gallery box (H)

   a.   Used on T1, T2, T3, T4, and T5

   b.   Editor selects one or more stories and specific media for each story; editor sets one story as the primary story

   c.   If more than one story, selected box will show gallery controls to move between story media

   d.   Box displays the media selected one at a time, be it a video, a slide show, or an MP3

   e.   Gallery is ordered by primary story first, then by Story.Published

   f.   OPEN ISSUE: Does video auto play? Do slideshows auto play?

Additional box editing storyboard management features:

- If a box has no content selected, it will not appear on the live view at all
- **Auto-populate buttons**
  - Used for filling in stories in parts of boxes
  - Pulls stories sorted by Story.Published, Story.Rank matching the category of primary story in box
- Story selection: The field for selecting a story should be an auto-suggest tool
  - Suggest should match on title
  - Suggestions should be ordered by Story.Published, Story.Rank
  - User can also enter in the NID directly and the system will associate to the correct story
  - Users can drag and drop stories between the story selection areas of different boxes on the storyboard

Working with Storyboards

General features:

- Storyboards have the following:
  - Name, used by the editorial team, shown internally
  - User last edited by
  - Last edited by date
  - Template
- Users can create new storyboards from scratch or by starting from an existing storyboard

  Create from:

  - When starting from existing storyboard, pre-fill in all stories from the copy from storyboard as applicable, based on box type
  - Any stories that don't fit into the new storyboard are dropped
  - The user must specify a new name for the storyboard

Scratch:

- Users must enter a name and select a built-in template
- After selection, they are taken to the storyboard editing screen

- Global auto-populate button

  - The global auto-populate button will allow a user to pre-fill in all available story selection fields based on the standard selection criteria
  - Pressing this button will fill in all empty story selection fields, in order from top to bottom, left to right, on the template, for box types that have story selection fields

- Saving

  - At the top of the storyboard edit screen is a Save button Manual saves are done in the background, via Ajax

  - Below the Save button is a text string that reports the last time it was saved
  - Storyboards should save automatically every five minutes in the background

- Publish Now button

  - The Publish Now button appears next to the Save button
  - Clicking this button opens up a pop-up with a drop-down and confirmation buttons
  - The drop-down includes the site home page and the section home pages, allowing the user to publish this storyboard at any time
  - If the currently edited storyboard is live, then the Publish Now button is disabled and text next to the button says "This storyboard is [live]." "Live" links to the public URL of the page using this storyboard and opens the link in a new window.
  - Storyboards cannot use template 6, which is a custom storyboard for blog home pages

The main ECP screen is a listing of all storyboards:

- List is sorted by live, then by storyboard last edited date
- Columns

  - Storyboard name

- Last updated
- Template
- Status—For setting new storyboards live
- Actions—Links for edit, clone, and preview

Change Order Request #1

Client Name

PROJECT NAME

Prepared on:	January 1, 2013
Version:	1.0 / January 1, 2013

ESTOR
CLIENT NAME
Attn: Client Contact
Address
City, State, ZIP
E-mail Address: email@domain.com
Telephone: 555-555-5555

UNT
Account Number / Name

VED BY
CONSULTANT NAME
Attn: Project Manager
Address
Address
City, State, ZIP
E-mail Address: email@domain.com
Telephone: 555-555-5555

RIPTION
Based on a series of two phone calls, and a screen sharing session to review the ap
tion, the project team requests the addition of the following features to the project
of work:

Description of change #1 (8 hours)

Description of change #2 (8 hours)

Description of change #3 (16 hours)

Etc.

Total: 32 hours

MPACT   The project cost will increase by $xx,xxx (32 hours @ $xxx/hour) to a total of $xxx,x

)ULE IMPACT   The project schedule may be extended by two weeks to accommodate this new tas

TIVE DATE   Change order is effective as of January 14, 2014.

Approvals:

Change Approved by: Change Approved by:
CLIENT NAME   CONSULTANT NAME

_____   _____
Authorized Signature   Authorized Signature

_____   _____
Name   Name

_____   _____
Title / Affiliation   Title / Affiliation

_____   _____
Date   Date

Project Training Agenda

Client Name

PROJECT NAME

1. Submitting Issues

If you encounter any kind of issue or problem, kindly send an e-mail to [your-issue-queue-intake@name.com].

If possible, include **steps to reproduce the issue** and a screen shot (you can paste a screen shot into Microsoft Word and attach that file to the e-mail).

2. Getting Help

The [Your Firm] team is here to help you with any questions you have during testing:

- [Your Name], email@name.com, 323-555-6901 x 100
- [Backup Person Name], email2@name.com, 323-555-6901 x 105

3. Accessing the Site

Main URL	http://stage.projecturl.com/
Pop-up username	[Project code or name shortened]
Pop-up password	apple (*Something easy to remember*)
Web site login URL	http://stage.projecturl.com/user
Web site username	E-mailed to you shortly after training
Web site password	E-mailed to you shortly after training

4. Training Outline

1. Site overview

2. Logging in

3. The current system

    a.   Roles: Student editors, student contributors

    b.   A Drupal node

    c.   Inactive components

4.   Administration navigation & user home page

5. Creating a basic story

6. How to edit a story

7. Advanced story posting

    a.   Changing the path

    b.   Tracking revisions

    c.   Posting to Twitter

    d.   Posting to Facebook

8.   Adding a pod cast

9.   Adding a map

10. Adding a slide show

11. Adding a video

12. Creating a blog post

13. Editorial Control Panel

    a.   About the ECP

    b.   Understanding storyboards and templates

    c.   Creating a storyboard

    d.   Making a storyboard live

    e.   Auto-populate

10.   Additional features

a. Wiki pages

b. Zeitgeist Dashboard

11. Questions?

12. Wrap-up & Next Steps

Testing Document

Client Name

PROJECT NAME

About the System

[Project Name] is a student-run online news media site that features original student-created content covering major news events. Think *Huffington Post* or *Daily Beast*.

URL: http://www.domain.com/

Username: [Project code or name shortened]

Password: apple (*Something easy to remember*)

(Include any additional log-in information needed by the tester.)

Important testing notes:

- For each item, enter either a ticket number or "COMPLETE" in the status column.
- Try to break the application with random input and unexpected behavior.
- Remember: If the system fails, it's the system's fault, not yours.
- **Confirm with [Project Team members] that the e-mail tool is in testing mode before sending any emails.**

Testing Checklist

Reference	Test	Status
	General	
1.	Create an account.	
2.	Use the Forgot Password link and confirm you can log in and reset your password.	

3.	Edit all parts of your registration information and confirm all data is saved correctly.	
4.	Create three new stories with long, multi-paragraph text.	
5.	Confirm line breaks are appearing correctly.	
6.	Confirm an automatic URL was created.	
7.	Insert a teaser break into a story and confirm the entered teaser is displayed on the home page.	
8.	Change the story title and confirm the URL does not change.	
9.	Manually change the URL for the story and confirm it's set.	
10.	Confirm that date-based URLs show a listing of stories (example: /news/2009/12/).	
11.	Confirm date-based URL pages are paginated.	
12.	Create several new discussion forum postings and confirm they appear.	
13.	Reply to several forum postings and confirm they appear.	
14.	Post several comments to a node and rate them as a logged-in user.	
15.	As an anonymous user, rate those comments you just rated and confirm the averages and rate counts appear correctly.	
16.	Verify that Google Analytics is tracking data on the stage site and production sites.	
17.	Submit a comment to a node that intentionally looks like spam. Confirm that CAPTCHA appears with the message "We're sorry, but the spam filter thinks your submission could be spam. Please complete the CAPTCHA."	
18.	For the spam test, confirm you can submit the comment with the correct CAPTCHA and you can't submit it with incorrect CAPTCHA.	
19.	Create a WordPress blog post and make a test post. Then create a story and blog entry on the site that	

		links to your blog post and confirm a pingback is received on your WordPress blog.	
	20.	Confirm that Google Analytics is tracking data for the site.	
	21.	Post several stories and confirm posts appear as expected and the URL is aliased by date (/yyyy/mm/title).	
	22.	Confirm that you have a user blog home page that lists your newly created content.	
	23.	Create some content and verify you can set specific keywords that appear in the source code of the node when created.	
	24.	Subscribe to a specific piece of content, an author, and a type of content. Make edits contact matching all three and confirm you get alerts about change.	
	25.	Post a story and confirm that a Tweet is created.	
	26.	Confirm you don't see Facebook or Twitter options on any content type except Story.	
	27.	Confirm that links for news categories and news tags are /news/categoryname and /tags/tagname.	
	28.	Confirm you can save information for custom profile fields like title and USC ID.	
	29.	"Watch" several nodes and make changes to them. Confirm you get alerts for the changes when you verify wanting e-mail notifications.	
	30.	Repeat the previous as an anonymous user.	
	31.	Create several posts with different MP3 files for pod casts. Confirm each MP3 attachment appears in a Flash pod cast player and works.	
	32.	Create and embed several Google Maps into stories. Be sure to set all of the properties for each map, and vary what you do. Confirm the maps appear correctly when the node is output.	
	33.	Create several event nodes. Confirm that each node's URL is hackable, showing the correct events for the date.	

34.	Create several different kinds of nodes and upload images to use in each node. Verify only the "uploads" directory is accessible, and not its parent directory.	
35.	Create a story on the site and a blog post on the testing blog (see project wiki page), and include bi-directional links to verify outbound and inbound pingbacks are working.	
36.	Create a story, and have it posted to Facebook (log in using the Facebook icon using your own FB account). Confirm the post goes to the wall of the page the module is set to.	
37.	Create several discussion forums and confirm postings work as expected.	
38.	Log in as a user of the role "student contributor" and create several blog posts. Confirm you can publish them and they appear in the blog home page for anonymous visitors.	
	Zeitgeist Dashboard	
39.	Identify a story in the Zeitgeist Dashboard "Most talked about stories" section that is not at the top, add enough comments to the story to make it move up a position, and reload the dashboard to confirm this is reflected.	
40.	Pick a term not in the "Top Searches" box and search for it 10 times. Confirm the term now appears on this box.	
41.	Click on several random tag, story, and Twitter links and confirm everything loads as expected.	
42.	Confirm each chart loads without error.	
43.	Log in and out of the site as several different users and confirm "Recently logged-in users" reflects this activity.	
	Rich Media	
44.	Create a Google Map, complete with custom shapes, position, and zoom, and embed it into a node. Create two additional nodes with two additional (different)	

	maps.	
45.	Create several wiki pages. Verify wiki syntax (Creole style) works (see http://www.wikicreole.org/wiki/EditPageHelp).	
46.	Create several stories and verify each of the formatting options available in the editor for the BODY field are preserved when the node is saved and viewed.	
	Editorial Control Panel	
47.	Using the stories you have created so far, set up a blank storyboard, populate every box, and make the storyboard live on the home page. Verify home page formatting, links, and media are correct.	
48.	Set up a new storyboard with a different template and complete the task described in the previous step. Set this as a new, live section home page.	
49.	Set up a new storyboard with a different template and complete the task described in the previous step. Set this as a new, live section home page.	
50.	Duplicate an existing template to create a new one, change three boxes, and post live. Confirm changes are set.	
51.	Set a RANK of 1 on several recent stories you added. Create a new blank storyboard and use the auto-populate feature. Confirm all stories are recent, and ones ranked 1 appear first.	
	Permissions Testing	
52.	Log in as a site editor and confirm you can only access ECP, user management, and blocks.	
53.	As a site editor, verify you cannot access any other Drupal admin functions.	
54.	Verify that anonymous cannot register on the site.	
55.	Log in as a contributor and confirm you cannot publish nodes and cannot access any Drupal administration page.	

Tested by (print name)

Signed   Date

Launch Checklist

Client Name

PROJECT NAME

Document Purpose: This document helps to ensure that the client's web site is launched according to best practices, and that all the little details that tend to get lost in the launch process are tracked and addressed.

Pre-Launch

1. Cross-Browser Check

Check all the top-level category pages and key secondary pages in the modern versions and one previous version of Firefox, IE, Safari, Chrome.

2. Basic or Advanced Web Accessibility Measures

By default, we perform basic accessibility enhancements, because it is the right thing to do. If the client has selected Section 508-compliance as part of Urban Insight's scope of services, then perform the advanced steps.

3. Forms Check

Confirm that some form of spam protection was installed during the initial site setup.

Confirm with the project manager who should receive e-mail notifications from the forms on the web site.

Test each form on the web site by submitting your own real and relevant contact information and asking the recipient to confirm receipt of the result form e-mail.

4. Graceful Degradation

The web site should work with JavaScript turned off. Using the Firefox developer toolbar, turn off JavaScript, and browse through five pages on the web site to ensure that it is still usable.

5. Print Style Sheet

We always now create a CSS print style for printing pages. If a user wants to print a page from a web site, she will typically only want the main content and not the navigation or extra design elements. A print-specific style sheet enables this printing style. Certain CSS elements, such as floats, do not print well.

6. Custom 404 Error Page

Build and configure a custom error page to display when pages are not found.

7. Favicon

A favicon brands the tab or window in which your web site is open in the user's browser. It is also saved with the bookmark so that users can easily identify pages from your web site. Design the icon that appears in the browser bar that appears when the site loads.

8. Page Titles

Ensure that web site pages have relevant and SEO-optimized page titles.

9. Home Page Meta Description

Ensure that the home page has a useful and SEO-optimized description.

10. Editor Control Panel

Ensure that the "control panel" that editors will see is usable, friendly, and includes all key functions editors will need.

11. Broadcast E-mail Integration

Ensure that your integration with third-party broadcast e-mail systems works and is configured correctly.

12. QA Review

Perform a final detailed Q/A review using your testing checklist. Get a new pair of eyes to browse through the web site.

13. Review Scope, Amendments, Change Orders

Review all the project documents and confirm that you have done everything you agreed to do, or schedule any remaining work so the client knows it is scheduled for after the launch.

14. Confirm Accounts

Confirm that all necessary accounts are created, and that accounts have the correct permissions.

Launch

15. DNS

Update DNS to point to the live site and/or switch the URL from the legacy site to the production site.

16. Send Launch E-mail

Send your client an e-mail confirming and congratulating them on the web site launch and next steps.

The launch of the web site may trigger a support period where you provide support for bug fixes and other issues related to the web site. For this reason, it is important to document the date the web site launched and reiterate this support window.

17. Domain and SSL Standardization

It is good practice to ensure that the web site has a single, uniform URL for every page, such as the domain.com forwards to www.domain.com. Ensure that SSL pages redirect to their non-SSL equivalent if you use a common Web root to prevent having two URLs for each page (https and http).

18. Analytics

Ensure that your analytics software is set up, configured, and working.

Set up automated monthly reports to be e-mailed to project contacts.

19. CMS Refinements

If you are using a content management system, such as WordPress, Drupal, etc., there are a number of post-launch optimizations and refinements that need to be made. For example, for launching a Drupal web site, there are 20 specific refinements that should be made for production web sites.

20. Automated Site Link Check

Run an automated check of all links on the web site.

21. Set Up Monitoring

If you are proactively monitoring your web site, set up your monitoring software/system, and determine who should be notified if there are problems.

22. Install SSL Certificate

If the site requires logins, install and configure an SSL certificate.

Confirm that there are no "errors" caused by displaying non-secure items on the page.

Post-Launch

23. Automated Processes/Cron

If your site requires automated processes to run to keep the site in good health, set up and configure these automated processes now.

24. Register for Maintenance

Create all documentation required for ongoing maintenance, and notify whoever performs maintenance that the site is now in production operations state. (For example, we have a different support team from our development team.)

25. Set Up Support Orientation

Set up a support orientation with your client.

26. Order Muffin Basket

Consider sending your client a small gift to congratulate them on the successful launch of their web site.

27. VIP Refinements

Some web sites require special handling, refinements, or optimizations. You can include those here. For example, maybe you will benchmark SEO placement or web site load performance, or perform some custom tuning.

28. Marketing

Go through your marketing checklist to make sure the world knows about your new web site.

Support Subscription Orientation

Client Name

PROJECT NAME

Purpose

- Introduce you to how Urban Insight provides ongoing support for your web site.

How to Request Support

- E-mail us (Preferred): support@yoursite.com
- Call us: 877-867-5309
- Fax us: 877-867-5310

What Happens Next?

- Request goes into our Case tracking system.
- Within four hours, a team member evaluates the request.
- If request can be resolved in less than two hours, we perform the work.
- Within eight business hours, request is completed.
- If more information is required, or the request requires more than two hours, we contact you with an estimate and timeline for completion.
- Case number and description appears on your monthly invoice.

How to Report a Bug or Problem

- What were you trying to do?
- What did you expect to happen?
- What actually happened?
- What browser, browser version, and operating system are you using? (For example: Firefox 4 on Mac OSX 10.6 or Internet Explorer 9 on Windows 7)

Introducing Your Support Team

- Bob Support
- Delyte Support

Authorized Callers

- Who is authorized to call on your behalf?
- Up to two contacts
- We need for each: Name, e-mail, telephone
- We need one security passphrase for your organization (Example: "The dog is in Kansas").

Software Support Subscription

- We perform security patches, other updates, and schedule patches.
- We schedule updates to be performed Monday through Thursday at an agreed-upon time between 9am and 4pm PT (to ensure maximum availability of [Your Firm] and client staff for 24 hours in the unlikely need of maximum support).
- We notify you when we will perform the update.
- We estimate two hours to perform the update.
- We perform the update and perform QA testing.

- We notify you when the update is complete.
- We encourage you to perform testing after each upgrade.

Let's Create Your Quality Assurance Plan

- Action 1: Visit the home page, confirm it loads.
- Action 2:
- Action 3:
- Action 4:
- Action 5:

Review Your Support Plan

Plan	
Monthly fee	
Support hours/month	
Drupal hosting	
Drupal updates	
Rate, additional hours	
Initial response time	
Web site monitoring	
24x7 Emergency coverage	

Web Site Monitoring (Optional)

- Would you like us to provide web site monitoring?

- We monitor the home page.
- Who should be notified (up to three emails)?
- By default, we will notify the authorized caller(s).

Emergency Support Options (Optional)

- Response on emergency events, 24x7, within 1 hour.
- Would you like us to provide emergency support?
- If so, let's define the emergency support steps. For example:
    - Step 1: Verify web site is down; attempt to log in to Drupal.
    - Step 2: Notify authorized callers via e-mail web site is offline.
    - Step 3: Contact hosting company to evaluate problem.
    - Step 4: Determine problem and recover web site.
    - Step 5: Perform quality-assurance checklist steps.
    - Step 6: Notify authorized callers via e-mail when web site is online.

Questions?

Weekly Checklist

This can be a simple text list in a recurring calendar item in a calendaring application or a to-do list in a checklist application.

1. Are there any outstanding client action items from last week that need follow-up?

2. Are there any meetings this week that need prep?

3. Check [Developer A]'s and [Developer B]'s previous week's hours allocation.

4. [Project A]: Review budget, update the project schedule, and schedule tasks for week.

5. [Project B]: Review budget, update the project schedule, and schedule tasks for week.

6. [Project C]: Review budget, update the project schedule, and schedule tasks for week.

7. Review tasks for [Developer A]; prep for check-in meeting.

8. Review tasks for [Developer B]; prep for check-in meeting.

9. Monthly: Send check-in e-mail to [Support Client A].

10. Monthly: Send check-in e-mail to [Support Client B].

11. Monthly: Recognize one team member for outstanding work with Amazon.com GiftCard.

I

Index

CPSIA information can be obtained
at www.ICGtesting.com
Printed in the USA
LVHW010528200722
723852LV00007B/269